10 Fantastically Hard SAT Vocabulary Practice Tests

Paul G Simpson IV

with the Staff of Test Professors

Acknowledgements

I would like to thank David Hao for yet another instance of hard work and dedication. Finally, thanks to all of our students, past and present, without whom this book would not have been possible.

10 Fantastically Hard SAT Vocabulary Practice Tests

SAT VOCABULARY PRACTICE TEST 1

Suggested Time: 5 minutes
8 Questions

> **Directions:** In context, choose the word(s) that fits the sentence best.

1. He not only disliked his nickname but -----
being called "Cooter" by his family and
friends.

   (A) razed (B) deposed (C) loathed
   (D) obfuscated (E) commenced

2. The sanitary worker, upon learning that he had
won the lottery, was not just happy but
absolutely ----- at the prospect of an affluent
future.

   (A) capacious (B) feckless (C) bellicose
   (D) amoral (E) gleeful

3. Although the child had expected to get into
trouble, he was surprised by the ferocity of his
parents' ----- and raving.

   (A) prattling (B) loathing (C) obfuscating
   (D) ranting (E) eulogizing

4. Raj maintained that his was not a whimsical
----- but a principled stubbornness born from
convictions.

   (A) obduracy (B) loathing (C) acrimony
   (D) eulogy (E) melancholy

5. Sylvia Plath fought a life-long battle with
depression, finally succumbing to ----- by
ending her life in 1963.

   (A) obduracy (B) panacea (C) equanimity
   (D) melancholy (E) ignominy

6. The voters were poised to vote on whether to
----- existing buildings or to ----- them and
construct an entirely new downtown area.

   (A) catalogue…endure
   (B) obfuscate…desiccate
   (C) commence…emend
   (D) revitalize…raze
   (E) eulogize…ensconce

7. The unused brain, like unexercised muscle, is
subject to ----- and decay.

   (A) evanescence (B) torpor (C) atrophy
   (D) discourse (E) virulence

8. The teacher urged her students to avoid -----,
hackneyed phrases not only for the benefit of
their writing but also for her own mental
health, as all things trite made her
disconsolate and -----.

   (A) pedestrian…morose
   (B) ambivalent…drab
   (C) galvanic…myopic
   (D) perspicuous…somnolent
   (E) hexed…providential

Suggested Time: 3 minutes
5 Questions

Directions: In context, choose the word(s) that fits the sentence best.

---

1. Only years after he had started to treat patients was the man discovered to be a -----, who had neither a license nor any medical knowledge.

   (A) dilettante   (B) neophyte   (C) prodigy
       (D) mercenary   (E) charlatan

2. At the time, the presidential candidate's promise not to raise taxes was peripheral to the central theme of his speech, and yet the issue became quite -----, a central theme, during the campaign after his opponent brought up his prior acceptance of tax hikes.

   (A) indomitable   (B) voracious   (C) paltry
       (D) apposite   (E) opulent

3. The diet gurus approach to weight loss was -----: one advocated the consumption of carbohydrates, while the others championed the eating of protein.

   (A) esoteric   (B) disparate   (C) diffident
       (D) haughty   (E) unobtrusive

4. Unable to confront the significant work ahead, the lawyer relegated all the case files to the corner of her office and instead focused on the relatively ----- matter of clipping her nails.

   (A) effusive   (B) curt   (C) clandestine
       (D) picayune   (E) aberrant

5. A scrutiny of the firm's finances revealed that it had been ----- with its expense accounts to the point that if it did not begin to ----- its resources immediately, then it would soon face insolvency.

   (A) diffident…cease
   (B) pompous…foil
   (C) curt…exasperate
   (D) petulant…protract
   (E) improvident…husband

Suggested Time: 4 minutes
6 Questions

Directions: In context, choose the word(s) that fits the sentence best.

1. Jennifer earned a slew of commendations from local and national organizations, each of which hailed her ----- devotion to animal rights.

   (A) profane   (B) magnanimous   (C) puckish
   (D) meek   (E) saturnine

2. After he lost his job, his house and his car, his friends were not astonished to find that he no longer his usual ----- and sanguine self.

   (A) benign   (B) indigent   (C) befuddled
   (D) ephemeral   (E) jovial

3. The error of the contractor, who built a house without a roof, was not a slight one that the homeowners could overlook but an ----- one that they noticed immediately.

   (A) ephemeral   (B) aloof   (C) ascetic
   (D) effusive   (E) egregious

4. Though now solely remembered for a pamphlet that ----- and chided the government, he was best known by his contemporaries for a ----- tract that sang the praises of coffee.

   (A) instigated…dreary
   (B) elucidated…waffling
   (C) quelled…pernicious
   (D) propitiated…jejune
   (E) upbraided…panegyric

5. After he made four egregious mistakes in the company's account books in less than a week, he was labeled as a ----- employee who would certainly lose his jobs.

   (A) remunerative   (B) gallant   (C) lugubrious
   (D) bungling   (E) austere

6. Jeong longed to prove that his zest for rock polishing was no ----- fascination but rather ----- passion that he would continue to pursue for years to come.

   (A) congenial…an abounding
   (B) puckish…a temperate
   (C) effusive…a transitory
   (D) fleeting…an abiding
   (E) pertinacious…a coy

Practice Test 1
Answer Key and Explanations

Section 1

1. (C) loathed
2. (E) gleeful
3. (D) ranting
4. (A) obduracy
5. (D) melancholy
6. (D) revitalize…raze
7. (C) atrophy
8. (A) pedestrian…morose

Section 2

1. (E) charlatan
2. (D) apposite
3. (B) disparate
4. (D) picayune
5. (E) improvident…husband

Section 3

1. (B) magnanimous
2. (E) jovial
3. (E) egregious
4. (E) upbraided…panegyric
5. (D) bungling
6. (D) fleeting…an abiding

Finding Your Percentile Rank

Raw score: Total Number Right – [Total Number Wrong ÷ 4] = _____

Raw Score	Percentile Rank
19	99
18	97
17	93
16	89
15	85
14	80
13	75
12	70
11	65
10	60
9	50
8	45
7	40
6	35
5	30
4	25
3	20
2	15
1	10
0	5
-1 or below	1 - 4

Identifying Strengths and Areas for Improvement

Go back to the test and circle the questions that you answered incorrectly. This review will allow you to see what vocabulary to study more closely. It will also allow you to see what word lists you need to review more carefully. You can also reference *Score-Raising Vocabulary Builder for ACT and SAT Prep*, a companion study guide and vocabulary workbook.

	Section 1	Section 2	Section 3
Generous			1
Weak	7		
Relevant		2	
Using a Lot		5	
Using a Little		5	
Ordinary	8		
Fake		1	
Inexperienced			5
Criticize / Scold	3		4
Praise			4
Dislike / Hate	1		
Cheerful	2		2
Depressed	5, 8		
Stubborn	4		
Different		3	
Regenerate	6		
Destroy	6		
Obvious			3
Insignificant		4	
Long-Lived			6
Short-Lived			6

Section 1

1. C (loathed: *hate*)

(A) razed: *destroy*
(B) deposed: *force*
(D) obfuscated: *unclear*
(E) commenced: *start*

2. E (gleeful: *cheerful*)

(A) capacious: *large*
(B) feckless: *unskilled*
(C) bellicose: *unfriendly*
(D) amoral: *wicked*

3. D (ranting: *criticize / scold*)

(A) prattling: *talkative*
(B) loathing: *hate*
(C) obfuscating: *unclear*
(E) eulogizing: *praise*

4. A (obduracy: *stubborn*)

(B) loathing: *hate*
(C) acrimony: *bitter*
(D) eulogy: *praise*
(E) melancholy: *depressed*

5. D (melancholy: *depressed*)

(A) obduracy: *stubborn*
(B) panacea: *cure-all*
(C) equanimity: *fair*
(E) ignominy: *shameful*

6. D (revitalize…raze: *regenerate…destroy*)

(A) catalogue…endure:
    record…long-lived
(B) obfuscate…desiccate:
    unclear…lose water
(C) commence…emend:
    start…make better
(E) eulogize…ensconce:
    praise…secure

7. C (atrophy: *weak*)

(A) evanescence: *short-lived*
(B) torpor: *lazy*
(D) discourse: *examine*
(E) virulence: *harmful*

8. A (pedestrian…morose: *ordinary…depressed*)

(B) ambivalent…drab:
    unclear…boring
(C) galvanic…myopic:
    exciting…unclear
(D) perspicuous…somnolent:
    clear…boring
(E) hexed…providential:
    unlucky…lucky

Section 2

1. E (charlatan: *fake*)

(A) dilettante: *amateur*
(B) neophyte: *inexperienced*
(C) prodigy: *skilled*
(D) mercenary: *concerned with objects*

2. D (apposite: *relevant*)

(A) indomitable: *strong*
(B) voracious : *greedy*
(C) paltry: *small*
(E) opulent: *rich / extravagant*

3. B (disparate: *different*)

(A) esoteric: *secret / difficult to understand*
(C) diffident: *shy*
(D) haughty: *arrogant*
(E) unobtrusive: *humble / not obvious*

4. D (picayune: *insignificant*)

(A) effusive: *talkative*
(B) curt: *tight-lipped*
(C) clandestine: *secret*
(E) aberrant: *different*

**5. E (improvident…husband:
    using a lot…using a little)**

(A) diffident…cease:
    shy…finish
(B) pompous…foil:
    arrogant…stop
(C) curt…exasperate:
    tight-lipped…make worse
(D) petulant…protract:
    unfriendly…make large

Section 3

1. B (magnanimous: *generous*)

(A) profane: *wicked*
(C) puckish: *unfriendly*
(D) meek: *humble*
(E) saturnine: *depressed*

2. E (jovial: *cheerful*)

(A) benign: *harmless*
(B) indigent: *poor*
(C) befuddled: *confused*
(D) ephemeral: *short-lived*

3. E (egregious: *obvious*)

(A) ephemeral: *short-lived*
(B) aloof: *arrogant*
(C) ascetic: *using a little*
(D) effusive: *talkative*

4. E (upbraided...panegyric:
   criticize...praise)

(A) instigated...dreary:
   start...boring
(B) elucidated...waffling:
   explain...unsure
(C) quelled...pernicious:
   stop...harmful
(D) propitiated...jejune:
   make better...boring

5. D (bungling: *inexperienced*)

(A) remunerative: *rich*
(B) gallant: *brave*
(C) lugubrious: *depressed*
(E) austere: *using a little*

6. D (fleeting...an abiding:
   short-lived...long-lived)

(A) congenial...an abounding:
   friendly...a lot
(B) puckish...a temperate:
   unfriendly...using a little
(C) effusive...a transitory:
   talkative...short-lived
(E) pertinacious...a coy:
   stubborn...shy

SAT VOCABULARY PRACTICE TEST 2

Suggested Time: 5 minutes
8 Questions

Directions: In context, choose the word(s) that fits the sentence best.

---

1. Moderate doses of vitamins may help to increase health; excessive doses, however, can be ----- and harmful.

   (A) evanescent (B) revitalizing (C) banal
        (D) toxic (E) acrid

2. When exposed to a surfeit of light, the pupils of the eye ----- and shrink; conversely, when there is a lack of light, the pupils -----.

   (A) ameliorate…incite
   (B) subvert…ebb
   (C) contract…dilate
   (D) elucidate…protract
   (E) desist…squander

3. Commoners opined that Catherine of Aragon remained regal during her difficulties of imprisonment and banishment, even as her critics in the royalty continued to ----- and deprecate her standing.

   (A) squander (B) fabricate (C) wheedle
        (D) lambaste (E) exult

4. The family was alerted to the fire by the bitter, ----- smell of smoke pouring from the kitchen.

   (A) desiccated (B) acrid (C) enduring
        (D) ensconced (E) fitful

5. His fervor for extreme skateboarding was ----- after he attempted a triple-flip 2880 trick and smashed his forehead directly on the sidewalk curb.

   (A) accrued (B) hailed (C) dilated
        (D) curbed (E) traduced

6. After completing her latest novel, the author was exhausted and sank into an extended -----.

   (A) bombast (B) nefariousness (C) torpor
        (D) panacea (E) rant

7. While published words may be ----- and survive millennia, spoken words are normally -----.

   (A) insuperable…iconoclastic
   (B) enduring…evanescent
   (C) banal…ensconced
   (D) antediluvian…profligate
   (E) tantamount…faltering

8. Without warning, the explorers found themselves in a ----- which left them stuck, unable to step either forward or backward.

   (A) catalogue (B) mosaic (C) quagmire
        (D) discourse (E) labyrinth

Suggested Time: 3 minutes
5 Questions

Directions: In context, choose the word(s) that fits the sentence best.

---

1. While his friends charged down the hiking trails, Pokey ----- casually down the mountain.

   (A) averted   (B) spurned   (C) stupefied
      (D) swaggered   (E) meandered

2. The criminal's rehearsed answers were truly -----, inept to the point that even the most rookie detective could have refuted his claims and caused him to change his story.

   (A) bowing   (B) dismayed   (C) hackneyed
      (D) petty   (E) feckless

3. In Michelle's memory, her elementary school had loomed large and -----; when she visited it during her spring break from college, however, the school seemed -----, almost miniscule.

   (A) exorbitant…bantam
   (B) capacious…diminutive
   (C) insatiable…multitudinous
   (D) blithe…austere
   (E) colossal…loquacious

4. After she discovered the cure for not one, but eight, common childhood diseases, she was considered not just competent but a ----- in the field of pediatrics.

   (A) tyro   (B) pauper   (C) sycophant
      (D) maven   (E) neophyte

5. The editor rejected the column as -----, marked by obscure paragraphs and ambiguous meaning.

   (A) wanton   (B) elliptical   (C) gargantuan
      (D) feckless   (E) bellicose

Suggested Time: 4 minutes
6 Questions

> **Directions:** In context, choose the word(s) that fits the sentence best.

1. Daniel's excuses for not turning his assignment were -----; he had different ones for all five of his professors and several more for his advisor.

   (A) sullen　(B) multitudinous　(C) quotidian
   　　(D) baleful　(E) auspicious

2. Rather than lead to a final agreement, the negotiator's last offer only angered the other party and reignited the long-standing ----- that had kept them apart for so many years.

   (A) paucity　(B) enmity　(C) inanity
   　　(D) candor　(E) zeal

3. When Leslie realized that her open, ----- campaign to receive a raise from her boss had failed, she switched tactics and began a ----- effort.

   (A) dubious…slothful
   (B) overt…clandestine
   (C) trenchant…flummoxed
   (D) myopic…quixotic
   (E) tonic…malapropos

4. No matter how many fawning compliments the child gave to his mother, she refused to succumb to such ----- and made it clear that her decision to ground him was ----- and firm.

   (A) flagging…dejected
   (B) inveigling…robust
   (C) allaying…audacious
   (D) bootlicking…provident
   (E) loathing…insuperable

5. For centuries the mule has been, alternately, decried and celebrated as the exemplar of a willful and ----- nature.

   (A) imperishable　(B) refractory　(C) exorbitant
   　　(D) capacious　(E) diminutive

6. The ----- rains of Phoenix, which rarely last for more than ten minutes, stand in stark contrast to the ----- rains of Bangladesh, which can last for months.

   (A) iniquitous…seasoned
   (B) ebullient…capricious
   (C) rapturous…jejune
   (D) pithy…adroit
   (E) transitory…unremitting

Practice Test 2
Answer Key and Explanations

Section 1

1. (D) toxic
2. (C) contract…dilate
3. (D) lambaste
4. (B) acrid
5. (D) curbed
6. (C) torpor
7. (B) enduring…evanescent
8. (C) quagmire

Section 2

1. (E) meandered
2. (E) feckless
3. (B) capacious…diminutive
4. (D) maven
5. (B) elliptical

Section 3

1. (B) multitudinous
2. (B) enmity
3. (B) overt…clandestine
4. (B) inveigling…robust
5. (B) refractory
6. (E) transitory…unremitting

Finding Your Percentile Rank

Raw score: Total Number Right – [Total Number Wrong ÷ 4] = _____

Raw Score	Percentile Rank
19	99
18	97
17	93
16	89
15	85
14	80
13	75
12	70
11	65
10	60
9	50
8	45
7	40
6	35
5	30
4	25
3	20
2	15
1	10
0	5
-1 or below	1 - 4

Identifying Strengths and Areas for Improvement

Go back to the test and circle the questions that you answered incorrectly. This review will allow you to see what vocabulary to study more closely. It will also allow you to see what word lists you need to review more carefully. You can also reference *Score-Raising Vocabulary Builder for ACT and SAT Prep*, a companion study guide and vocabulary workbook.

	Section 1	Section 2	Section 3
Large		3	
Small		3	
To Wander		1	
To Stop	5		
Bitter	4		
Make Large	2		
Make Small	2		
Indifferent / Lazy	6		
Harmful	1		
To Criticize / Scold	3		
Long-Lived	7		6
Short-Lived	7		6
Stuck	8		
Unskilled		2	
Experienced		4	
Difficult to Understand		5	
A Lot			1
Hate			2
Obvious			3
Secret			3
Flatter			4
Strong			4
Stubborn			5

Section 1

1. D (toxic: *harmful*)

(A) evanescent: *short-lived*
(B) revitalizing: *regenerate*
(C) banal: *clichéd*
(E) acrid: *bitter*

2. C (contract...dilate:
**   *make small...make large*)**

(A) ameliorate...incite:
    make better...start
(B) subvert...ebb:
    make worse...make small
(D) elucidate...protract:
    explain...make large
(E) desist...squander:
    stop...using a lot

3. D (lambaste: *to criticize / scold*)

(A) squander: to *waste*
(B) fabricate: *false / lying*
(C) wheedle: *to flatter*
(E) exult: *praise*

4. B (acrid: *bitter*)

(A) desiccated: *lose water*
(C) enduring: *long-lived*
(D) ensconced: *secure*
(E) fitful: *unsteady*

5. D (curbed: *stop*)

(A) accrued: *make large*
(B) hailed: *praise*
(C) dilated: *make large*
(E) traduced: *insult*

6. C (torpor: *lazy / indifferent*)

(A) bombast: *arrogant*
(B) nefariousness: *wicked*
(D) panacea: *cure-all*
(E) rant: *criticize / scold*

7. B (enduring...evanescent:
**   *long-lived...short-lived*)**

(A) insuperable...iconoclastic:
    strong...different / odd
(C) banal...ensconced:
    clichéd...secure
(D) antediluvian...profligate:
    old...using a lot
(E) tantamount...faltering:
    equivalent...unsteady

8. C (quagmire: *stuck*)

(A) catalogue: *to record*
(B) mosaic: *made from small pieces*
(D) discourse: *examine*
(E) labyrinth: *maze*

Section 2

1. E (meandered: *wandered*)

(A) averted: *avoid*
(B) spurned: *reject*
(C) stupefied: *surprised*
(D) swaggered: *arrogant*

2. E (feckless: *unskilled*)

(A) bowing: *obedient*
(B) dismayed: *depressed*
(C) hackneyed: *clichéd*
(D) petty: *insignificant*

3. B (capacious...diminutive: *large...small*)

(A) exorbitant...bantam:
    using a lot...little
(C) insatiable...multitudinous:
    greedy...a lot
(D) blithe...austere:
    cheerful...using a little
(E) colossal...loquacious:
    large...talkative

4. D (maven: *experienced*)

(A) tyro: *inexperienced*
(B) pauper: *poor*
(C) sycophant: *flatter*
(E) neophyte: *inexperienced*

5. B (elliptical: *difficult to understand*)

(A) wanton: *using a lot*
(C) gargantuan: *large*
(D) feckless: *inexperienced*
(E) bellicose: *unfriendly*

Section 3

1. B (multitudinous: *a lot*)

(A) sullen: *depressed*
(C) quotidian: *ordinary / clichéd*
(D) baleful: *harmful*
(E) auspicious: *lucky*

2. B (enmity: *hate*)

(A) paucity: *a little*
(C) inanity: *stupid*
(D) candor: *honest*
(E) zeal: *passionate*

3. B (overt...clandestine: *obvious...secret*)

(A) dubious...slothful:
    questioning...lazy
(C) trenchant...flummoxed:
    smart...confused
(D) myopic...quixotic:
    unclear...different
(E) tonic...malapropos:
    exciting...irrelevant

4. B (inveigling…robust:
   flatter…strong)

(A) flagging…dejected:
   stop…depressed
(C) allaying …audacious:
   make better…brave
(D) bootlicking…provident:
   flatter…lucky
(E) loathing…insuperable:
   hate…strong

5. B (refractory: *stubborn*)

(A) imperishable: *long-lived*
(C) exorbitant: *using a lot*
(D) capacious: *large*
(E) diminutive: *small*

6. E (transitory…unremitting:
   short-lived…long-lived)

(A) iniquitous…seasoned:
   wicked…experienced
(B) ebullient…capricious:
   cheerful…impulsive
(C) rapturous…jejune:
   cheerful…inexperienced
(D) pithy…adroit:
   tight-lipped…skilled

SAT VOCABULARY PRACTICE TEST 3

Suggested Time: 5 minutes
8 Questions

Directions: In context, choose the word(s) that fits the sentence best.

1. The notary public refused to ----- Myron's document because of the suspicion that its signature had been forged and its content spurious.

   (A) fabricate   (B) gainsay   (C) taunt
   (D) eulogize   (E) validate

2. Grace ran an economical household in which prodigality was abhorred and ----- was cherished.

   (A) parsimony   (B) ambiguity   (C) exacerbation
   (D) dejection   (E) immoderation

3. The corporation countered charges of ----- by releasing a list of its charitable donations.

   (A) equanimity   (B) obduracy   (C) ignominy
   (D) avarice   (E) banality

4. Contrary to earlier pictures of the universe constructed by physicists, newer theories propound not a universe of intermittent creation but one of ----- birth.

   (A) unceasing   (B) pedestrian   (C) deft
   (D) puerile   (E) meek

5. In order to gain trust and perform their jobs well, undercover agents must have the ability to deceive and ----- the targets of their investigations.

   (A) protract   (B) impede   (C) terminate
   (D) dissemble   (E) institute

6. The villagers strung rows of chili peppers not to decorate their homes but to ----- the vegetables, drying them for later use.

   (A) distend   (B) catalogue   (C) desiccate
   (D) depose   (E) commemorate

7. His knowledge of medieval history was ----- and encyclopedic; his common sense, on the other hand, was ----- if not altogether absent.

   (A) trenchant…consummate
   (B) prodigious…infinitesimal
   (C) banal…enduring
   (D) profligate…atrophied
   (E) prudent…fitful

8. Although the room was ----- with toys, which seemed to cover every square inch of the floor, they could not satiate the ----- children who continued to demand more and more.

   (A) replete…fallacious
   (B) refuted…jaunty
   (C) idle…insatiable
   (D) teeming…covetous
   (E) captivated…ardent

Suggested Time: 3 minutes
5 Questions

> **Directions:** In context, choose the word(s) that fits the sentence best.

1. By the time of his college graduation, Juvy's lucky baby blanket had been worn -----.

   (A) fallow (B) lurid (C) mercurial
       (D) threadbare (E) ravenous

2. Finally presented with the chance to ask out the girl of his dreams, Peter was so ----- in her presence that he could not utter a single word.

   (A) mundane (B) flummoxed (C) malignant
       (D) unequivocal (E) drab

3. Moe would never have considered attending the comic convention; he was neither a ----- reader of comic books nor a strong supporter of comic-based films.

   (A) noxious (B) myopic (C) haphazard
       (D) staunch (E) fledgling

4. After listening to the debate, Barney came to appreciate that the issue of land management, which he had previously thought to be -----, was actually a central issue that was ----- to the well-being of the society.

   (A) orthogonal…ascetic
   (B) material…gargantuan
   (C) bona fide…impudent
   (D) tangential…apposite
   (E) usurious…self-effacing

5. Unlike her ----- predecessor, Sophia preferred to a management style that was less ----- and more congenial and friendly.

   (A) stupendous…idle
   (B) bellicose…pugnacious
   (C) profligate…flummoxed
   (D) recondite…divergent
   (E) mettlesome…sumptuous

Suggested Time: 4 minutes
6 Questions

Directions: In context, choose the word(s) that fits the sentence best.

1. The trust between them did not instantly vanish but rather ----- slowly over a period of years.

   (A) catalogued   (B) emended   (C) ensconced
       (D) corroded   (E) prattled

2. Known for a capricious nature, Patricia did not surprise her friends when she abandoned her ----- and reticent stance at the party in favor of a ----- one.

   (A) retiring…garrulous
   (B) inexorable…surmountable
   (C) glowering…capricious
   (D) bashful…hackneyed
   (E) tenacious…robust

3. Used to the meek advances of former business acquaintances, she was embarrassed in the face of the ----- approach employed by the newest potential partner, who refused to acquiesce to even the most minor demand.

   (A) ebullient   (B) apathetic   (C) tangential
       (D) incredulous   (E) rigid

4. Contemporaries of the great Dr. Johnson uniformly described his as ----- person who loved nothing more than joking and laughing with companions.

   (A) a cantankerous   (B) an astute   (C) a jocund
       (D) a candid   (E) an effusive

5. Sally's ----- spending spree, evidence of which was readily available in her outrageous credit card statements, left her ----- and in desperate need of cash.

   (A) exorbitant…wanting
   (B) deferential…lavish
   (C) bungling…quotidian
   (D) picayune…maladroit
   (E) ineluctable…demoralized

6. Though the worker was threatened with immediate dismissal if he disclosed his company's illegal activities, she remained ----- in the face of these threats and leaked the details in a press conference.

   (A) remunerative   (B) stalwart   (C) lugubrious
       (D) parsimonious   (E) altruistic

Practice Test 3
Answer Key and Explanations

Section 1

1. (E) validate
2. (A) parsimony
3. (D) avarice
4. (A) unceasing
5. (D) dissemble
6. (C) desiccate
7. (B) prodigious...infinitesimal
8. (D) teeming...covetous

Section 2

1. (D) threadbare
2. (B) flummoxed
3. (D) staunch
4. (D) tangential...apposite
5. (B) bellicose...pugnacious

Section 3

1. (D) corroded
2. (A) retiring...garrulous
3. (E) rigid
4. (C) a jocund
5. (A) exorbitant...wanting
6. (B) stalwart

Finding Your Percentile Rank

Raw score: Total Number Right − [Total Number Wrong ÷ 4] = _____

Raw Score	Percentile Rank
19	99
18	97
17	93
16	89
15	85
14	80
13	75
12	70
11	65
10	60
9	50
8	45
7	40
6	35
5	30
4	25
3	20
2	15
1	10
0	5
-1 or below	1 - 4

Identifying Strengths and Areas for Improvement

Go back to the test and circle the questions that you answered incorrectly. This review will allow you to see what vocabulary to study more closely. It will also allow you to see what word lists you need to review more carefully. You can also reference *Score-Raising Vocabulary Builder for ACT and SAT Prep*, a companion study guide and vocabulary workbook.

	Section 1	Section 2	Section 3
To Argue For	1		
Large	7		
Small	7		
Using a Lot			5
Using a Little	2		
Make Worse			1
Greedy	3, 8		
False / Lying	5		
Confused		2	
To Lose Water	6		
A Lot	8		
A Little			5
Relevant		4	
Irrelevant		4	
Long-Lived	4		
Friendly			2
Unfriendly		5	
Stubborn			3
Poor		1	
Shy			2
Cheerful			4
Strong		3	6

Section 1

1. E (validate: *argue for*)

(A) fabricate: *false / lying*
(B) gainsay: *argue against*
(C) taunt: *mocking*
(D) eulogize: *praise*

2. A (parsimony: *using a little*)

(B) ambiguity: *unclear*
(C) exacerbation: *make worse*
(D) dejection: *depressed*
(E) immoderation: *using a lot*

3. D (avarice: *greedy*)

(A) equanimity: *fair*
(B) obduracy: *stubborn*
(C) ignominy: *shameful*
(E) banality: *clichéd*

4. A (unceasing: *long-lived*)

(B) pedestrian: *clichéd*
(C) deft: *skilled*
(D) puerile: *inexperienced*
(E) meek: *obedient*

5. D (dissemble: *false / lying*)

(A) protract: *make large*
(B) impede: *stop*
(C) terminate: *finish*
(E) institute: *start*

6. C (desiccate: *lose water*)

(A) distend: *make large / swell*
(B) catalogue: *record*
(D) depose: *force*
(E) commemorate: *respect*

7. B (prodigious…infinitesimal: *large…small*)

(A) trenchant…consummate:
    relevant…finish
(C) banal…enduring:
    clichéd…long-lived
(D) profligate…atrophied:
    using a lot…weak
(E) prudent…fitful:
    cautious…unsteady

8. D (teeming…covetous: *a lot…greedy*)

(A) replete…fallacious:
    a lot…false
(B) refuted…jaunty:
    argue against…cheerful
(C) idle…insatiable:
    lazy…greedy
(E) captivated…ardent:
    cheerful…passionate

Section 2

1. D (threadbare: *poor*)

(A) fallow: *empty*
(B) lurid: *sensational*
(C) mercurial: *unsteady*
(E) ravenous: *greedy*

2. B (flummoxed: *confused*)

(A) mundane: *ordinary*
(C) malignant: *harmful*
(D) unequivocal: *sure*
(E) drab: *boring*

3. D (staunch: *strong*)

(A) noxious: *harmful*
(B) myopic: *unclear*
(C) haphazard: *impulsive*
(E) fledgling: *inexperienced*

4. D (tangential…apposite:
    irrelevant…relevant)

(A) orthogonal…ascetic:
    irrelevant…using a little
(B) material…gargantuan:
    relevant…large
(C) bona fide…impudent:
    true…arrogant
(E) usurious…self-effacing:
    using a lot…shy

5. B (bellicose…pugnacious:
    unfriendly…unfriendly)

(A) stupendous…idle:
    large…lazy / indifferent
(C) profligate…flummoxed:
    using a lot…confused
(D) recondite…divergent:
    difficult to understand…different
(E) mettlesome…sumptuous:
    brave…rich / extravagant

Section 3

1. D (corroded: *make worse*)

(A) catalogued: *to record*
(B) emended: *make better*
(C) ensconced: *secure*
(E) prattled: *talkative*

2. A (retiring…garrulous:
    shy…friendly)

(B) inexorable…surmountable:
    strong…weak
(C) glowering…capricious:
    unfriendly…impulsive
(D) bashful…hackneyed:
    shy…clichéd
(E) tenacious…robust:
    stubborn…strong

3. E (rigid: *stubborn*)

(A) ebullient: *cheerful*
(B) apathetic: *indifferent*
(C) tangential: *irrelevant*
(D) incredulous: *questioning / doubtful*

4. C (jocund: *cheerful*)

(A) a cantankerous: *unfriendly*
(B) an astute: *smart*
(D) a candid: *honest*
(E) an effusive: *talkative*

5. A (exorbitant…wanting:
   ***using a lot…a little*)**

(B) deferential…lavish:
   obedient…rich / extravagant
(C) bungling…quotidian:
   unskilled…clichéd
(D) picayune…maladroit:
   insignificant…unskilled
(E) ineluctable…demoralized:
   sure…depressed

6. B (stalwart: *strong*)

(A) remunerative: *rich*
(C) lugubrious: *depressed*
(D) parsimonious: *using a little*
(E) altruistic: *generous*

SAT VOCABULARY PRACTICE TEST 4

Suggested Time: 5 minutes
8 Questions

> **Directions:** In context, choose the word(s) that fits the sentence best.

1. Unlike her colleagues, who were not as -----
   in their criticisms, Evelyn remained frank in
   her assessment of the shortcomings of the
   company's management.

   (A) sanguine   (B) prattling   (C) refined
       (D) blunt   (E) unwieldy

2. Not small to begin with, Marya's debts
   became positively ----- after she lost her job
   and her assets were seized as part of a police
   investigation.

   (A) gargantuan   (B) paltry   (C) gawky
       (D) glum   (E) acquiescent

3. The insurgents failed to ----- the president,
   who thereafter retained his position for
   decades.

   (A) ensconce   (B) atrophy   (C) revitalize
       (D) emend   (E) depose

4. Archeologists still speculate how the ancient
   natives of Easter Island could fashion such
   ---- structures, some of which stand 12-feet
   high and weigh over 14 tons, with only the
   most basic and crude tools

   (A) languid   (B) digressive   (C) cynical
       (D) lavish   (E) monolithic

5. The recent findings of evolutionary
   biologists indicate the rapidity of the
   progression of dogs' evolution from wild and
   feral beasts to tame and ----- creatures that
   obey the commands of humans.

   (A) dejected   (B) dreary   (C) gawky
       (D) docile   (E) flagrant

6. Extreme malnutrition often marks its victims
   with sunken cheeks and swollen, ----- bellies.

   (A) obsequious   (B) prattling   (C) fitful
       (D) distended   (E) infinitesimal

7. Their recent attempt to ----- their expenses by
   only eating at home and never going
   shopping was a constant struggle because it
   ran contrary to their wanton, -----
   personalities.

   (A) approbation…lucrative
   (B) castigate…altruistic
   (C) dilate…avaricious
   (D) husband…improvident
   (E) hail…impregnable

8. In consideration of the family's -----
   circumstances, exemplified by their bank
   account balance of fifty-two cents, it decided
   to empty its retirement and college funds.

   (A) exiguous   (B) sententious   (C) furtive
       (D) anomalous   (E) diffident

Suggested Time: 3 minutes
5 Questions

Directions: In context, choose the word(s) that fits the sentence best.

---

1. When polite refusals did not stop the telemarketer, the woman forcefully ----- his two-for-one offer on dog tuxedoes.

   (A) parodied   (B) swaggered   (C) disquieted
        (D) buttressed   (E) spurned

2. The teacher was impressed by Serenity's ----- responses, ones that showed true insight and originality, particularly for a student so young.

   (A) chastened   (B) surreptitious   (C) keen
        (D) meretricious   (E) quibbling

3. Anthropologists describe the Kalangi tribe of the Amazon as a ----- treasure trove of culture, customs and traditions that hearken back thousands of years.

   (A) veritable   (B) genial   (C) fractious
        (D) dejected   (E) tenuous

4. In the business world, Eric had a well-deserved reputation for ----- in acquiring competitors; in his private life, however, he was known as ----- man who supported several local charities.

   (A) extirpation…a waffling
   (B) voraciousness…an altruistic
   (C) appeasement…a myopic
   (D) somnolence…a jejune
   (E) rapacity…a perspicuous

5. In political campaigns it has become almost standard procedure for a candidate to attempt to ----- his opponent's reputation, in the hopes that such calumny will guarantee a victory.

   (A) squelch   (B) billow   (C) besmirch
        (D) blandish   (E) panegyrize

Suggested Time: 4 minutes
6 Questions

Directions: In context, choose the word(s) that fits the sentence best.

1. The manager ----- the investors with false claims of easy money and early retirement.

   (A) atrophied (B) beguiled (C) faltered
   (D) emended (E) loathed

2. The foreign minister continued to fight charges of ----- spending, even after published reports revealed that he had spent more than five million dollars on collectible plates in just the last three months alone.

   (A) furtive (B) heterogeneous (C) immoderate
   (D) reticent (E) haughty

3. The emperor of Rome never realized that his overextended architecture of government was ----- and susceptible to collapse, until the Visigoths delivered the final and decisive blow.

   (A) rickety (B) stalwart (C) morose
   (D) austere (E) garrulous

4. The intransigence of the dog, which continued to stubbornly chew on the furniture, was broken by the lure of treats, which almost immediately rendered the dog ----- to the wishes of its owners.

   (A) unassailable (B) biddable (C) callow
   (D) heedless (E) languid

5. As a recent Ivy-league graduate, Yuri believed that her job prospects were ----- when, in fact, the shrinking economy made them ----- and uncertain.

   (A) feeble…incessant
   (B) prodigious…hallowed
   (C) stout…tenuous
   (D) austere…jaunty
   (E) magnanimous…menial

6. After impromptu kudos from local townspeople, the firefighter received ----- from the mayor, who held an official ceremony at city hall.

   (A) a palaver (B) a befuddlement
   (C) a confutation (D) a lampoon
   (E) an encomium

Practice Test 4
Answer Key and Explanations

Section 1

1. (D) blunt
2. (A) gargantuan
3. (E) depose
4. (E) monolithic
5. (D) docile
6. (D) distended
7. (D) husband…improvident
8. (A) exiguous

Section 2

1. (E) spurned
2. (C) keen
3. (A) veritable
4. (B) voraciousness…an altruistic
5. (C) besmirch

Section 3

1. (B) beguiled
2. (C) immoderate
3. (A) rickety
4. (B) biddable
5. (C) stout…tenuous
6. (E) an encomium

Finding Your Percentile Rank

Raw score: Total Number Right – [Total Number Wrong ÷ 4] = _____

Raw Score	Percentile Rank
19	99
18	97
17	93
16	89
15	85
14	80
13	75
12	70
11	65
10	60
9	50
8	45
7	40
6	35
5	30
4	25
3	20
2	15
1	10
0	5
-1 or below	1 - 4

Identifying Strengths and Areas for Improvement

Go back to the test and circle the questions that you answered incorrectly. This review will allow you to see what vocabulary to study more closely. It will also allow you to see what word lists you need to review more carefully. You can also reference *Score-Raising Vocabulary Builder for ACT and SAT Prep*, a companion study guide and vocabulary workbook.

	Section 1	Section 2	Section 3
To Reject		1	
To Force	3		
Smart		2	
Strong			5
Weak			3
Make Large / Swell	6		
Insult		5	
Poor	8		
Uncertain			5
Large	2, 4		
Generous		4	
Greedy		4	
Obedient	5		4
Using a Lot	7		2
Using a Little	7		
Praise			6
True / Honest	1	3	
False / Lying			1

Section 1

1. D (blunt: *honest*)

(A) sanguine: *cheerful*
(B) prattling: *talkative*
(C) refined: *experienced*
(E) unwieldy: *unskilled*

2. A (gargantuan: *large*)

(B) paltry: *small*
(C) gawky: *inexperienced*
(D) glum: *depressed*
(E) acquiescent: *obedient*

3. E (depose: *force*)

(A) ensconce: *secure*
(B) atrophy: *weak*
(C) revitalize: *regenerate*
(D) emend: *make better*

4. E (monolithic: *large*)

(A) languid: *lazy*
(B) digressive: *irrelevant*
(C) cynical: *questioning*
(D) lavish: *rich / extravagant*

5. D (docile: *obedient*)

(A) dejected: *depressed*
(B) dreary: *boring*
(C) gawky: *unskilled*
(E) flagrant: *obvious*

6. D (distended: *make large / swell*)

(A) obsequious: *flatter*
(B) prattling: *talkative*
(C) fitful: *unsteady*
(E) infinitesimal: *small*

7. D (husband...improvident:
**   *using a little...using a lot*)**

(A) approbation... lucrative:
    praise...rich
(B) castigate...altruistic:
    criticize...generous
(C) dilate... avaricious:
    make large...greedy
(E) hail... impregnable:
    praise...strong

8. A (exiguous: *poor / inadequate*)

(B) sententious: *tight-lipped*
(C) furtive: *secret*
(D) anomalous : *different*
(E) diffident: *shy*

Section 2

1. E (spurned: *to reject*)

(A) parodied: *mock*
(B) swaggered: *arrogant*
(C) disquieted: *upset*
(D) buttressed: to *argue for / support*

2. C (keen: *smart*)

(A) chastened: *criticize / scold*
(B) surreptitious: *secret*
(D) meretricious: *false / lying*
(E) quibbling: *unfriendly*

3. A (veritable: *true*)

(B) genial: *friendly*
(C) fractious: *stubborn*
(D) dejected: *depressed*
(E) tenuous: *unsure*

4. B (voraciousness...an altruistic: *greedy...generous*)

(A) extirpation...a waffling:
  stop...unsure
(C) appeasement...a myopic:
  make better...unclear
(D) somnolence...a jejune:
  boring...boring
(E) rapacity...a perspicuous:
  greedy...clear

5. C (besmirch: *insult*)

(A) squelch: *stop*
(B) billow: *make large*
(D) blandish: *flatter*
(E) panegyrize: *praise*

Section 3

1. B (beguiled: *false / lying*)

(A) atrophied: *weak*
(C) faltered: *stopped*
(D) emended: *make better*
(E) loathed: *hate*

2. C (immoderate: *using a lot*)

(A) furtive: *secret*
(B) heterogeneous: *different*
(D) reticent: *shy*
(E) haughty: *arrogant*

3. A (rickety: *weak*)

(B) stalwart: *strong*
(C) morose: *depressed*
(D) austere: *using a little*
(E) garrulous: *friendly*

4. B (biddable: *obedient*)

(A) unassailable: *strong*
(C) callow: *inexperienced*
(D) heedless: *impulsive*
(E) languid: *lazy / indifferent*

5. C (stout...tenuous: *strong...unsure*)

(A) feeble...incessant:
  weak...long-lived
(B) prodigious...hallowed:
  large...blessed
(D) austere...jaunty:
  using a little...cheerful
(E) magnanimous...menial:
  generous...humble

6. E (an encomium: *praise*)

(A) a palaver: *talkative*
(B) a befuddlement: *confused*
(C) a confutation: *argue against*
(D) a lampoon : *mocking*

SAT VOCABULARY PRACTICE TEST 5

Suggested Time: 5 minutes
8 Questions

> **Directions:** In context, choose the word(s) that fits the sentence best.

1. After a victory over his nemesis in table tennis, Phil could not think of any other way to properly ----- his joy than to pump his fists in the air while singing "We are the Champions."

   (A) repudiate   (B) dupe   (C) fabricate
      (D) punctuate   (E) curtail

2. Oliver believed that the ----- that the dejected townspeople felt was, in large part, due to the community's ----- architecture, which featured identical homes painted identical colors behind identical front lawns.

   (A) auspiciousness…coy
   (B) dreariness…monotonous
   (C) haphazardness…evanescent
   (D) sententiousness…unquenchable
   (E) self-effacement…magnanimous

3. Unlike the ----- atmosphere of the team's home court, the opponent's court was hostile, surrounded by fans who wished them only ill-will and defeat.

   (A) peripheral   (B) genial   (C) dubious
      (D) obdurate   (E) noxious

4. In contrast to teammates who regularly participated in vigorous workouts, Chris often skipped training and soon gained a reputation as indolent and -----.

   (A) coy   (B) slothful   (C) aloof
      (D) docile   (E) capricious

5. Before the highest court in the land, the honest whistle-blower ----- that she had seen her superiors act in a corrupt and illicit manner that violated the law.

   (A) execrated   (B) scoffed   (C) avowed
      (D) prevaricated   (E) abated

6. Although the audience had long stopped listening, the actor continued to ----- about the people he wished to thank.

   (A) prattle   (B) falter   (C) rant
      (D) depose   (E) consummate

7. In comparison with the ----- seven-term senator who opposed him, the first-term senator was a political -----.

(A) stolid…charlatan
(B) bombastic…prodigy
(C) odious…mercenary
(D) seasoned…neophyte
(E) invincible…iconoclast

8. The charlatan passed as an expert by ----- his explanations until his listeners gave up on trying to understand them and accepted them as the truth.

(A) ensconcing (B) atrophying (C) beguiling
(D) faltering   (E) obfuscating

Suggested Time: 3 minutes
5 Questions

Directions: In context, choose the word(s) that fits the sentence best.

1. Tabloids lure their readers with ----- articles, stories that include ghastly, sensational details.

   (A) repugnant   (B) lurid   (C) raucous
      (D) aggregate   (E) veracious

2. Thomas More refused to ----- to Henry VIII, who demanded absolute obedience, even when More knew that one simple act of flattery would ensure the safety of himself and his family.

   (A) accrue   (B) curb   (C) inaugurate
      (D) placate   (E) kowtow

3. No matter how many flatteries she directed its way, Skye's attempt to ----- the dog into following her commands failed miserably.

   (A) wheedle   (B) augment   (C) adulterate
      (D) flag   (E) fabricate

4. The returning soldiers may not have expected commendation or ----- upon their return, but they certainly did not expect the ----- and disdain that they faced.

   (A) tenaciousness…animadversion
   (B) condemnation…obsequiousness
   (C) urbanity…facility
   (D) éclat…improvidence
   (E) exaltation…excoriation

5. The sporting world was shocked when the -----, who had never previously fought in a professional match, knocked out the veteran champion in the second round.

   (A) maven   (B) sage   (C) radical
      (D) tyro   (E) sycophant

Suggested Time: 4 minutes
6 Questions

Directions: In context, choose the word(s) that fits the sentence best.

1. After he failed to answer a single test question correctly, Dave lost his confidence and -----.

   (A) trepidation   (B) accolades   (C) swagger
   (D) effacement   (E) parsimony

2. Julia was ----- by nature, spending modestly even while her friends purchased gifts and clothes frequently.

   (A) aloof   (B) monumental   (C) abstentious
   (D) capricious   (E) malleable

3. Derby did not realize the ----- nature of his video-games until the many hours spent conquering them caused a drop in his grades and a school suspension for too many absences.

   (A) avaricious (B) diminutive (C) remunerative
   (D) insidious   (E) valiant

4. Never known for -----, Tina surprised her colleagues when she abandoned her normal intransigence and instead became ----- to all of their requests.

   (A) serendipity…refractory
   (B) meekness…amenable
   (C) indisputability…garrulous
   (D) opaqueness…abiding
   (E) lugubriousness…usurious

5. The politician's heinous and ----- acts, when they were revealed by the press, completely eclipsed her public image as a ----- and virtuous person.

   (A) nefarious…coy
   (B) garrulous…choleric
   (C) curt… taciturn
   (D) reprobate …beatific
   (E) captivated… chaste

6. Mike swore that he would no longer procrastinate and ----- that, from that point forward, he would always turn in his assignments in a timely fashion.

   (A) abhorred   (B) compressed   (C) reproved
   (D) averred   (E) waxed

Practice Test 5
Answer Key and Explanations

Section 1

1. (D) punctuate
2. (B) dreariness…monotonous
3. (B) genial
4. (B) slothful
5. (C) avowed
6. (A) prattle
7. (D) seasoned…neophyte
8. (E) obfuscating

Section 2

1. (B) lurid
2. (E) kowtow
3. (A) wheedle
4. (E) exaltation…excoriation
5. (D) tyro

Section 3

1. (C) swagger
2. (C) abstentious
3. (D) insidious
4. (B) meekness…amenable
5. (D) reprobate …beatific
6. (D) averred

Finding Your Percentile Rank

Raw score: Total Number Right – [Total Number Wrong ÷ 4] = _____

Raw Score	Percentile Rank
19	99
18	97
17	93
16	89
15	85
14	80
13	75
12	70
11	65
10	60
9	50
8	45
7	40
6	35
5	30
4	25
3	20
2	15
1	10
0	5
-1 or below	1 - 4

Identifying Strengths and Areas for Improvement

Go back to the test and circle the questions that you answered incorrectly. This review will allow you to see what vocabulary to study more closely. It will also allow you to see what word lists you need to review more carefully. You can also reference *Score-Raising Vocabulary Builder for ACT and SAT Prep*, a companion study guide and vocabulary workbook.

	Section 1	Section 2	Section 3
Sensational		1	
To Argue For	5		6
To Emphasize	1		
Arrogant			1
Unclear	8		
Boring	2		
Indifferent / Lazy	4		
Praise		4	
To Criticize / Scold		4	
Using a Little			2
To Flatter		2, 3	
Friendly	3		
Experienced	7		
Inexperienced	7	5	
Talkative	6		
Blessed			5
Wicked			5
Harmful			3
Humble			4
Obedient			4

Section 1

1. D (punctuate: *emphasize*)

(A) repudiate: *argue against*
(B) dupe: *stupid*
(C) fabricate: *false / lying*
(E) curtail: *make small*

**2. B (dreariness...monotonous:
boring...boring)**

(A) auspiciousness...coy:
lucky...shy
(C) haphazardness...evanescent:
impulsive...short-lived
(D) sententiousness...unquenchable:
tight-lipped...greedy
(E) self-effacement...magnanimous:
shy...generous

3. B (genial: *friendly*)

(A) peripheral: *irrelevant*
(C) dubious: *questioning*
(D) obdurate: *stubborn*
(E) noxious: *harmful*

4. B (slothful: *lazy / indifferent*)

(A) coy: *shy*
(C) aloof: *arrogant*
(D) docile: *obedient*
(E) capricious: *impulsive*

5. C (avowed: *argue for*)

(A) execrated: *hate*
(B) scoffed: *mocking*
(D) prevaricated: *lying*
(E) abated: *stop*

6. A (prattle: *talkative*)

(B) falter: *unsteady*
(C) rant: *criticize / scold*
(D) depose: *force*
(E) consummate: *finish*

**7. D (seasoned...neophyte:
experienced...inexperienced)**

(A) stolid...charlatan:
unemotional...fake
(B) bombastic...prodigy:
arrogant...skilled
(C) odious...mercenary:
hate...concerned with objects
(E) invincible...iconoclast:
strong...different / odd

8. E (obfuscating: *unclear*)

(A) ensconcing: *secure*
(B) atrophying: *weak*
(C) beguiling: *false / lying*
(D) faltering: *unsteady*

Section 2

1. B (lurid: *sensational*)

(A) repugnant: *offensive*
(C) raucous: *loud*
(D) aggregate: *together*
(E) veracious: *true / honest*

2. E (kowtow: *flatter*)

(A) accrue: *make large*
(B) curb: *stop*
(C) inaugurate: *start*
(D) placate: *make better*

3. A (wheedle: *flatter*)

(B) augment: *make large*
(C) adulterate: *make worse*
(D) flag: *stop*
(E) fabricate: *false / lying*

4. E (exaltation…excoriation: *praise…criticize / scold*)

(A) tenaciousness…animadversion:
  stubborn…hate
(B) condemnation…obsequiousness:
  criticize…flatter
(C) urbanity…facility:
  experienced…skilled
(D) éclat…improvidence:
  cheerful…using a lot

5. D (tyro: *inexperienced*)

(A) maven: *experienced*
(B) sage: *smart*
(C) radical: *original*
(E) sycophant: *flatter*

Section 3

1. C (swagger: *arrogant*)

(A) trepidation: *afraid*
(B) accolades: *praise*
(D) effacement: *erase*
(E) parsimony: *using a little*

2. C (abstentious: *using a little*)

(A) aloof: *arrogant*
(B) monumental: *large*
(D) capricious: *impulsive*
(E) malleable: *obedient*

3. D (insidious: *harmful*)

(A) avaricious: *greedy*
(B) diminutive: *small*
(C) remunerative: *rich*
(E) valiant: *brave*

4. B (meekness…amenable:
   ***humble…obedient*)**

(A) serendipity…refractory:
   lucky…stubborn
(C) indisputability…garrulous:
   unfriendly…friendly
(D) opaqueness…abiding:
   unclear…long-lived
(E) lugubriousness…usurious:
   depressed…using a lot

5. D (reprobate …beatific:
   ***wicked…blessed*)**

(A) nefarious…coy:
   wicked…shy
(B) garrulous… choleric:
   friendly…unfriendly
(C) curt… taciturn:
   tight-lipped…tight-lipped
(E) captivated… chaste:
   cheerful…blessed

6. D (averred: *argue for*)

(A) abhorred: *hate*
(B) compressed: *make small*
(C) reproved: *criticize*
(E) waxed: *make large*

SAT VOCABULARY PRACTICE TEST 6

Suggested Time: 5 minutes
8 Questions

Directions: In context, choose the word(s) that fits the sentence best.

1. The candidate ----- her campaign with a large fund-raising dinner filled with supporters.

   (A) emended   (B) razed   (C) catalogued
       (D) loathed   (E) commenced

2. In contrast to her seemingly docile appearance, Minnie was ----- mountaineer who had already climbed seven of the world's ten tallest mountains.

   (A) a ductile   (B) an intrepid   (C) a melancholy
       (D) a jejune   (E) a hapless

3. The pain from her broken ribs caused Selma to sleep only -----, waking off-and-on throughout the night.

   (A) inexorably   (B) stolidly   (C) trenchantly
       (D) fitfully   (E) beguilingly

4. The video game makers walked a very fine line in production, as they feared that a paucity of the games would anger customers that could not acquire the title, while a ----- of them would lower prices.

   (A) forte   (B) monotony   (C) consummation
       (D) dearth   (E) glut

5. The dictator's suppression and murder of his own people was universally criticized as -----, and his later refusal to let them be buried honorably as -----.

   (A) infernal…profane
   (B) docile…obstinate
   (C) coy…jocund
   (D) fiendish…taciturn
   (E) inimical…impeccable

6. Although she encountered several dangerous ----- along the way, Susan neither stumbled nor ----- in her pursuit of women's rights.

   (A) quagmires…commenced
   (B) charlatans…deposed
   (C) labyrinths…emended
   (D) neophytes...beguiled
   (E) pitfalls…faltered

7. The idea of a heliocentric universe so ----- the accepted doctrine of the time, that its author stipulated that its widespread publication be delayed until after his death.

   (A) hallowed   (B) augmented   (C) controverted
       (D) distended   (E) manifested

8. The wolf's snarled lip and dripping mouth made its edaciousness -----.

   (A) fledged   (B) acceding   (C) novice
       (D) innovative   (E) patent

Suggested Time: 3 minutes
5 Questions

Directions: In context, choose the word(s) that fits the sentence best.

---

1. Priya credited her brilliant success to her determination and ----- in pursuing her goals.

   (A) anachronism   (B) parody   (C) culpability
       (D) raucousness   (E) tenacity

2. While Summer thought her office duties boring and -----, she also understood that this initial opportunity would lead to more galvanizing opportunities.

   (A) gargantuan   (B) inept   (C) belligerent
       (D) iniquitous   (E) mundane

3. The lawyer's desire for wealth never ----- even after it became evident that his salary would never rise to a level approximating those of his far more successful peers.

   (A) disdained   (B) perpetuated   (C) averred
       (D) commenced   (E) ebbed

4. The defense attorney argued that the presence of her client near the crime scene was clearly ----- and should not be considered material by either the judge or the jury.

   (A) orthogonal   (B) acceding   (C) fledged
       (D) decrepit   (E) indomitable

5. Amose liked to joke that he grew up in ----- that provided him everything that he could ever have wanted and that sheltered him not only from the experience of, but even the thought of -----.

   (A) a remonstration…largess
   (B) a cornucopia…privation
   (C) an auspiciousness…transience
   (D) a famine…penuriousness
   (E) a facility…insolence

Suggested Time: 4 minutes
6 Questions

> **Directions:** In context, choose the word(s) that fits the sentence best.

1. Wilde was a popular at parties, where his abundant ----- never failed to spread merriment and ----- among his fellow guests.

   (A) witticisms…mirth
   (B) lampoons...blight
   (C) volubility…quiescence
   (D) mercurialness…respite
   (E) cacophony…remission

2. When the car's dashboard light went off, Frankie dismissed it as a ----- matter; only when his engine completely dropped out of his car three weeks later did he realize the light's significance.

   (A) seasoned   (B) languorous   (C) trifling
   (D) covetous   (E) parsimonious

3. In their early accounts, the conquistadors wrote breathlessly of how the New World ----- with natural resources, the quantity of which they promised would make the Spanish monarchs rich.

   (A) waned   (B) dissembled   (C) truckled
   (D) abounded   (E) abominated

4. His parents were -----, confused as they rarely had been before, by Adam's lackadaisical and ----- attitude towards his senior thesis, which he required in order to graduate and commence his college career.

   (A) insipid…unstinting
   (B) addled…otiose
   (C) lionhearted…wanton
   (D) miserly…bantam
   (E) befuddled…fugacious

5. Unaccustomed to having wants that could not be met, the family found itself crippled by the severe ----- that resulted from the famine and economic collapse of the country.

   (A) doltishness   (B) fervidness   (C) antipathy
   (D) privation   (E) fidelity

6. Elina decided not only to no longer ----- to her little brother, whom she had previously fawned over, but also to ----- his power over her servile parents.

   (A) truckle…stifle
   (B) squelch…inveigle
   (C) foreshorten…reprove
   (D) fabricate…herald
   (E) wheedle…squander

Practice Test 6
Answer Key and Explanations

Section 1

1. (E) commenced
2. (B) an intrepid
3. (D) fitfully
4. (E) glut
5. (A) infernal…profane
6. (E) pitfalls…faltered
7. (C) controverted
8. (E) patent

Section 2

1. (E) tenacity
2. (E) mundane
3. (E) ebbed
4. (A) orthogonal
5. (B) a cornucopia…privation

Section 3

1. (A) witticisms…mirth
2. (C) trifling
3. (D) abounded
4. (B) addled…otiose
5. (D) privation
6. (A) truckle…stifle

Finding Your Percentile Rank

Raw score: Total Number Right – [Total Number Wrong ÷ 4] = _____

Raw Score	Percentile Rank
19	99
18	97
17	93
16	89
15	85
14	80
13	75
12	70
11	65
10	60
9	50
8	45
7	40
6	35
5	30
4	25
3	20
2	15
1	10
0	5
-1 or below	1 - 4

Identifying Strengths and Areas for Improvement

Go back to the test and circle the questions that you answered incorrectly. This review will allow you to see what vocabulary to study more closely. It will also allow you to see what word lists you need to review more carefully. You can also reference *Score-Raising Vocabulary Builder for ACT and SAT Prep*, a companion study guide and vocabulary workbook.

	Section 1	Section 2	Section 3
To Stop			6
To Argue Against	7		
To Start	1		
Insignificant			2
Stubborn		1	
Confused			4
A Lot	4	5	3
A Little		5	5
Harmful	6		
Ordinary		2	
Wicked	5		
Humorous			1
Cheerful			1
Brave	2		
Make Small		3	
To Flatter			6
Irrelevant		4	
Obvious	8		
Unsteady	3, 6		
Lazy			4

Section 1

1. E (commenced: *start*)

(A) emended: *make better*
(B) razed: *destroyed*
(C) catalogued: *to record*
(D) loathed: *hate*

2. B (intrepid: *brave*)

(A) a ductile: *obedient*
(C) a melancholy: *depressed*
(D) a jejune: *boring*
(E) a hapless: *unlucky*

3. D (fitfully: *unsteady*)

(A) inexorably: *stubborn*
(B) stolidly: *unemotional*
(C) trenchantly: *relevant*
(E) beguilingly: *false / lying*

4. E (glut: *a lot*)

(A) forte: *skill*
(B) monotony: *boring*
(C) consummation: *finish*
(D) dearth: *a little*

5. A (infernal…profane: *wicked…wicked*)

(B) docile…obstinate: *obedient…stubborn*
(C) coy…jocund: *shy…cheerful*
(D) fiendish…taciturn: *wicked…tight-lipped*
(E) inimical…impeccable: *unfriendly…blessed*

6. E (pitfalls…faltered: *harmful…unsteady*)

(A) quagmires…commenced: *stuck…start*
(B) charlatans…deposed: *fake…force*
(C) labyrinths…emended: *maze…make better*
(D) neophytes...beguiled: *inexperienced…false / lying*

7. C (controverted: *argue against*)

(A) hallowed: *blessed*
(B) augmented: *make large*
(D) distended: *make large*
(E) manifested: *obvious*

8. E (patent: *obvious*)

(A) fledged: *experienced*
(B) acceding: *obedient*
(C) novice: *inexperienced*
(D) innovative: *original*

Section 2

1. E (tenacity: *stubborn*)

(A) anachronism: *old*
(B) parody: *mocking*
(C) culpability: *worthy of blame*
(D) raucousness: *loud*

2. E (mundane: *ordinary*)

(A) gargantuan: *large*
(B) inept: *unskilled*
(C) belligerent: *unfriendly*
(D) iniquitous: *wicked*

3. E (ebbed: *make small*)

(A) disdained: *hate*
(B) perpetuated: *long-lived*
(C) averred: *argue for*
(D) commenced: *start*

4. A (orthogonal: *irrelevant*)

(B) acceding: *obedient*
(C) fledged: *experienced*
(D) decrepit: *weak*
(E) indomitable: *strong*

5. B (a cornucopia…privation: *a lot…a little*)

(A) a remonstration…largess:
    criticize…generous
(C) an auspiciousness…transience:
    lucky…short-lived
(D) a famine…penuriousness:
    a little…poor
(E) a facility…insolence:
    skilled…arrogant

Section 3

1. A (witticisms…mirth: *humorous…cheerful*)

(B) lampoons...blight:
    mocking…destroyed
(C) volubility…quiescence:
    talkative…stopped
(D) mercurialness…respite:
    unsteady…rest
(E) cacophony…remission:
    loud…retreat

2. C (trifling: *insignificant*)

(A) seasoned: *experienced*
(B) languorous: *lazy / indifferent*
(D) covetous: *greedy*
(E) parsimonious: *using a little*

3. D (abounded: *a lot*)

(A) waned: *make small*
(B) dissembled: *false / lying*
(C) truckled: *flatter*
(E) abominated: *hate*

4. B (addled…otiose: *confused…lazy*)

(A) insipid…unstinting:
    stupid…generous
(C) lionhearted…wanton:
    brave…using a lot
(D) miserly…bantam:
    greedy…small
(E) befuddled…fugacious:
    confused…short-lived

5. D (privation: *a little / insufficient***)**

(A) doltishness: *stupid*
(B) fervidness: *passionate*
(C) antipathy: *hate*
(E) fidelity: *true / honest*

6. A (truckle...stifle:
   ***flatter...stop*)**

(B) squelch...inveigle:
   stop...flatter
(C) foreshorten...reprove:
   make small...criticize / scold
(D) fabricate...herald:
   false / lying...praise
(E) wheedle...squander:
   flatter...using a lot

SAT VOCABULARY PRACTICE TEST 7

Suggested Time: 5 minutes
8 Questions

> **Directions:** In context, choose the word(s) that fits the sentence best.

1. The country's economy was not ----- by a paucity of currency but rather from ----- of it, which devalued its currency and led to spiraling devaluation and inflation.

    (A) demystified…an execration
    (B) equivocated…an apathy
    (C) bedeviled…a glut
    (D) mollified…a reiteration
    (E) reserved…a forte

2. Primarily motivated by ----- and greed, the man assumed the role of a ----- who would flatter the rich in order to gain some of their money.

    (A) avarice…toady
    (B) pestilence…boor
    (C) gawkiness…pontificator
    (D) capriciousness…glutton
    (E) sullenness…pauper

3. The bureaucracy was -----, filled with complex entanglements and intricate procedures.

    (A) antediluvian (B) labyrinthine (C) nefarious
    (D) banal (E) prodigious

4. Unlike the mirthful calls of the nightingale, the ----- sounds of the dingo have been known to cause melancholy in those who live in the animals' vicinity.

    (A) lugubrious
    (B) docile
    (C) pompous
    (D) disparate
    (E) esoteric

5. After the corporation spent over two million dollars on remodeling its C.E.O.'s bathroom, critic accused it of ----- spending which far exceeded moderate expectations.

    (A) profligate (B) trite (C) benign
        (D) destitute (E) malleable

6. Tennyson's greatest poem, "In Memoriam," is an ----- that mourns the death of his friend, Arthur Henry Hallam.

    (A) acrimony (B) evanescence (C) eulogy
        (D) iconoclast (E) obduracy

7. After spending a lifetime organizing and -----
butterfly species, the professor left it to his
students to ----- his yet unfinished work.

(A) desiccating…prattle
(B) revitalizing…loathe
(C) emending…obfuscate
(D) cataloguing…consummate
(E) deposing…endure

8. Upon the publication of the 4,562-page novel,
critics chastened its author for ----- and
contended that the same story could have and
should have been told in 45 pages.

(A) vacillation (B) malignancy (C) capaciousne
(D) prolixity   (E) consummation

Suggested Time: 3 minutes
5 Questions

Directions: In context, choose the word(s) that fits the sentence best.

1. Sancho remained a ----- friend who stood by Don no matter how difficult the experience.

   (A) steadfast   (B) lurid   (C) mercurial
      (D) quiescent   (E) culpable

2. The committee's finding confirmed that the fire did not ----- the destruction of the house but rather followed the initial explosion which truly caused its ruin.

   (A) debunk   (B) instigate   (C) substantiate
      (D) compress   (E) reprove

3. The United States held ----- negotiations with the foreign administration, fearing that open publicity would deter a successful agreement.

   (A) gallant   (B) egregious   (C) sub-rosa
      (D) prodigal   (E) malevolent

4. Charles' parents congratulated him with a new house after he finally passed his CPA exam, making him ----- member of the family of accountants.

   (A) a fatuous   (B) a myriad   (C) an ebullient
      (D) a bona fide   (E) an apathetic

5. The number of students in the college -----, as it hired prestigious new professors and gained a reputation for a demanding, quality education.

   (A) assuaged   (B) waxed   (C) terminated
      (D) abated   (E) prevaricated

Suggested Time: 4 minutes
6 Questions

Directions: In context, choose the word(s) that fits the sentence best.

1. In order to ----- her excuse for missing homework, Cammy brought in a videotape of her Chihuahua chewing and eating her report.

   (A) disquiet (B) spurn (C) edify
      (D) buttress (E) efface

2. The students, stuck in the middle of calculus class, were ----- and flummoxed by the sudden appearance of not only a circus clown but also a singing baby elephant.

   (A) nonplussed (B) perpetuated
      (C) consummated (D) staunched
         (E) propitiated

3. Kevin's moves on the basketball court could never be mistaken for -----, though their awkward force often served him well and led to many easy baskets.

   (A) befuddled (B) ephemeral (C) incessant
      (D) deft (E) exorbitant

4. The army commended the soldier for valor, citing her courage in the face of enemy fire and her ----- act of rescuing civilians on the field of battle.

   (A) prodigious (B) copious (C) inept
      (D) mettlesome (E) ravening

5. Apart from his regular consumption of seven meals a day, he gained a reputation for ----- after it was discovered that he also consumed more than fifteen hamburgers in one sitting.

   (A) edaciousness (B) platitudes (C) facility
      (D) haphazardness (E) ebullience

6. Though he personally considered the councilwoman's views ----- and insipid, he did respect her as a savvy politician whose ----- maneuvers had allowed her to rise quickly to prominence.

   (A) spartan...gregarious
   (B) doltish...canny
   (C) fugacious...carping
   (D) grandiloquent...sainted
   (E) flyspeck...adamant

Practice Test 7
Answer Key and Explanations

Section 1

1. (C) bedeviled…a glut
2. (A) avarice…toady
3. (B) labyrinthine
4. (A) lugubrious
5. (A) profligate
6. (C) eulogy
7. (D) cataloguing…consummate
8. (D) prolixity

Section 2

1. (A) steadfast
2. (B) instigate
3. (C) sub-rosa
4. (D) a bona fide
5. (B) waxed

Section 3

1. (D) buttress
2. (A) nonplussed
3. (D) deft
4. (D) mettlesome
5. (A) edaciousness
6. (B) doltish…canny

Finding Your Percentile Rank

Raw score: Total Number Right – [Total Number Wrong ÷ 4] = _____

Raw Score	Percentile Rank
19	99
18	97
17	93
16	89
15	85
14	80
13	75
12	70
11	65
10	60
9	50
8	45
7	40
6	35
5	30
4	25
3	20
2	15
1	10
0	5
-1 or below	1 - 4

Identifying Strengths and Areas for Improvement

Go back to the test and circle the questions that you answered incorrectly. This review will allow you to see what vocabulary to study more closely. It will also allow you to see what word lists you need to review more carefully. You can also reference *Score-Raising Vocabulary Builder for ACT and SAT Prep*, a companion study guide and vocabulary workbook.

	Section 1	Section 2	Section 3
To Start		2	
To Finish	7		
To Record	7		
Constant		1	
Confused	1		2
Secret		3	
Depressed	4		
Make Large		5	
Using a Lot	5		
To Flatter	2		
Praise	6		
Complex	3		
Talkative	8		
A Little			
A Lot	1		
Smart			6
Stupid			6
Greedy	2		5
True / Honest		4	
Support			1
Skilled			3
Brave			4

Section 1

1. C (bedeviled...glut:
   confused...a lot)

(A) demystified...an execration:
   explain...hate
(B) equivocated...an apathy:
   unsure...indifferent
(D) mollified...a reiteration:
   make better...emphasize
(E) reserved...a forte:
   shy...skilled

2. A (avaricious...toady:
   greedy...flatter)

(B) pestilence...boor:
   harmful...unfriendly
(C) gawkiness...pontificator:
   unskilled...arrogant
(D) capriciousness...glutton:
   impulsive...using a lot
(E) sullenness...pauper:
   depressed...poor

3. B (labyrinthine: *complex*)

(A) antediluvian: *old*
(C) nefarious: *wicked*
(D) banal: *clichéd*
(E) prodigious: *large*

4. A (lugubrious: *depressed*)

(B) docile: *obedient*
(C) pompous: *arrogant*
(D) disparate: *different*
(E) esoteric: *secret / difficult to understand*

5. A (profligate: *using a lot*)

(B) trite: *clichéd*
(C) benign: *harmless*
(D) destitute: *poor*
(E) malleable: *obedient*

6. C (eulogy: *praise*)

(A) acrimony: *bitter*
(B) evanescence: *short-lived*
(D) iconoclast: *different / odd*
(E) obduracy: *stubborn*

7. D (cataloguing...consummate:
   to record...finish)

(A) desiccating...prattle:
   lose water...talkative
(B) revitalizing...loathe:
   regenerate...hate
(C) emending...obfuscate:
   make better...unclear
(E) deposing...endure:
   force...long-lived

8. D (prolixity: *talkative*)

(A) vacillation: *unsure*
(B) malignancy: *harmful*
(C) capaciousness: *large*
(E) consummation: *finish*

Section 2

1. A (steadfast: *constant*)

(B) lurid: *sensational*
(C) mercurial: *unsteady*
(D) quiescent: *stopped*
(E) culpable: *worthy of blame*

2. B (instigate: *start*)

(A) debunk: *argue against*
(C) substantiate: *argue for*
(D) compress: *make small*
(E) reprove: *criticize / scold*

3. C (sub-rosa: *secret*)

(A) gallant: *brave*
(B) egregious: *obvious*
(D) prodigal: *using a lot*
(E) malevolent: *wicked*

4. D (bona fide: *true / honest*)

(A) a fatuous: *stupid*
(B) a myriad: *a lot*
(C) an ebullient: *cheerful*
(E) an apathetic: *indifferent*

5. B (wane: *make small*)

(A) assuaged: *make better*
(C) terminated: *finish*
(D) abated: *stop*
(E) prevaricated: *lying*

Section 3

1. D (buttress: *argue for / support*)

(A) disquiet: *chaos*
(B) spurn: *reject*
(C) edify: *instruct*
(E) efface: *erase*

2. A (nonplussed: *confused*)

(B) perpetuated: *long-lived*
(C) consummated: *finish*
(D) staunched: *stop*
(E) propitiated: *make better*

3. D (deft: *skilled*)

(A) befuddled: *confused*
(B) ephemeral: *short-lived*
(C) incessant: *long-lived*
(E) exorbitant: *using a lot*

4. D (mettlesome: *courageous*)

(A) prodigious: *large*
(B) copious: *a lot*
(C) inept: *unskilled*
(E) ravening: *greedy*

5. A (edaciousness: *greedy*)

(B) platitudes: *clichéd*
(C) facility: *skilled*
(D) haphazardness: *impulsive*
(E) ebullience: *cheerful*

6. B (doltish…canny:
   stupid…smart)

(A) spartan…gregarious:
   using a little…friendly
(C) fugacious…carping:
   short-lived…unfriendly
(D) grandiloquent…sainted:
   arrogant…blessed
(E) flyspeck…adamant:
   little…stubborn

SAT VOCABULARY PRACTICE TEST 8

Suggested Time: 5 minutes
8 Questions

> **Directions:** In context, choose the word(s) that fits the sentence best.

1. Upon her admission to the rehabilitation facility, the head counselor clearly ----- the rules that she had to follow in order to stay in the program.

   (A) rebutted (B) exposited (C) disdained
       (D) foiled (E) debased

2. After she failed the bar exam for the fourth time, Noellia was downright ----- about her prospects of ever becoming a practicing attorney.

   (A) tonic (B) myopic (C) assured
       (D) stalwart (E) glum

3. When the country was attacked, the president ----- himself in a high-security bunker location.

   (A) faltered (B) ensconced (C) corroded
       (D) distended (E) prattled

4. French leaders thought the Maginot Line, a series of fortifications that stretched for 943 miles, would forever thwart any German offensive and make France -----.

   (A) belligerent (B) sagacious (C) unassailable
       (D) frank (E) nefarious

5. Non-governmental groups decried the administration's decision to cut taxes as -----, one made in ignorance of the true realities that confronted the country.

   (A) demure (B) nettlesome (C) diabolical
       (D) jovial (E) obtuse

6. Even in the face of rude and hostile questioners, Mrs. Poise maintained her ----- and provided polite and even-keeled responses.

   (A) obsequiousness (B) obduracy
     (C) iconoclasm (D) bombast
       (E) equanimity

7. Kathy believed Robitussin was a -----: a cure-all for everything from colds to shattered bones.

   (A) panacea   (B) virulence   (C) discourse
      (D) mosaic   (E) quagmire

8. The investigators immediately ascertained, upon examining the fingerprints and the driver's license left at the scene, that the robbery was not the work of ----- thieves but rather that of ----- amateurs.

   (A) altruistic…fledgling
   (B) avaricious…impregnable
   (C) refined…callow
   (D) decrepit…acceding
   (E) seasoned…avant-garde

Suggested Time: 3 minutes
5 Questions

Directions: In context, choose the word(s) that fits the sentence best.

---

1. Foods that one culture finds disgusting and ----- are often considered delicacies in another.

   (A) lithe   (B) unprecedented   (C) blighted
       (D) repugnant   (E) threadbare

2. The invention of the printing press ----- an unintended explosion of available information throughout the kingdom, as news soon became much more readily available.

   (A) abominated   (B) heralded   (C) excoriated
       (D) perverted   (E) distended

3. Though they were both police officers, they held ----- views on prisons as one believed their primary purpose to be punitive and the other, corrective.

   (A) consecrated   (B) divergent   (C) rapturous
       (D) lugubrious   (E) impuissant

4. No matter how ----- the manuscript before her, the editor read each and every dull word before her as a matter of professional duty.

   (A) docile   (B) whimsical   (C) jejune
       (D) adroit   (E) avant-garde

5. Sara was a consummate actress whose very skill allowed her to look ----- while prevaricating and to look ----- even as she told the truth.

   (A) ineluctable…inept
   (B) candid…meretricious
   (C) pellucid…reckless
   (D) galvanic…acquiescent
   (E) quotidian…caviling

Suggested Time: 4 minutes
6 Questions

> **Directions:** In context, choose the word(s) that fits the sentence best.

1. Despite his best efforts to destroy them, Kafka could not ----- all traces of his personal correspondence.

   (A) meander　(B) efface　(C) stupefy
   　(D) swagger　(E) aggregate

2. His relatives were shocked at his ----- home, which was filled with the newest appliances, since he had recently asked them for money and claimed that he earned very little as an assistant manager.

   (A) scant　(B) munificent　(C) incontrovertible
   　(D) sumptuous　(E) fallacious

3. Alan argued that his recent decision to become a vegetarian was not at all ----- to the current discussion on the early textiles of ancient Mesopotamia.

   (A) immaterial　(B) cogent　(C) commodious
   　(D) intractable　(E) malignant

4. The recent economic downturn has caused alarm within philanthropic circles, which have watched the bankruptcies of several charities and have called for government intervention before more ----- institutions slip into insolvency.

   (A) laconic　(B) loquacious　(C) eleemosynary
   　(D) malevolent　(E) inept

5. No matter that Darim's experience in forestry was -----, her ----- determination to succeed allowed her to not only master but also excel in the highest ranks of the Parks service.

   (A) pertinacious…assured
   (B) banal…limpid
   (C) paltry…prodigious
   (D) petty…soporific
   (E) feeble…appraising

6. The burglars fled after they broke into a house only to be confronted by the -----, sinister look of two dogs that seemed ready to cause them harm.

   (A) discursive　(B) cynical　(C) baleful
   　(D) adamant　(E) trite

Practice Test 8
Answer Key and Explanations

Section 1

1. (B) exposited
2. (E) glum
3. (B) ensconced
4. (C) unassailable
5. (E) obtuse
6. (E) equanimity
7. (A) panacea
8. (C) refined…callow

Section 2

1. (D) repugnant
2. (B) heralded
3. (B) divergent
4. (C) jejune
5. (B) candid…meretricious

Section 3

1. (B) efface
2. (D) sumptuous
3. (B) cogent
4. (C) eleemosynary
5. (C) paltry…prodigious
6. (C) baleful

Finding Your Percentile Rank

Raw score: Total Number Right – [Total Number Wrong ÷ 4] = _____

Raw Score	Percentile Rank
19	99
18	97
17	93
16	89
15	85
14	80
13	75
12	70
11	65
10	60
9	50
8	45
7	40
6	35
5	30
4	25
3	20
2	15
1	10
0	5
-1 or below	1 - 4

Identifying Strengths and Areas for Improvement

Go back to the test and circle the questions that you answered incorrectly. This review will allow you to see what vocabulary to study more closely. It will also allow you to see what word lists you need to review more carefully. You can also reference *Score-Raising Vocabulary Builder for ACT and SAT Prep*, a companion study guide and vocabulary workbook.

	Section 1	Section 2	Section 3
Erase			1
To Explain	1		
Fair	6		
Offensive		1	
True / Honest		5	
False / Lying		5	
Secure	3		
Praise		2	
Stupid	5		
Depressed	2		
Different		3	
Rich			2
Strong	4		
Boring		4	
Experienced	8		
Inexperienced	8		
Relevant			3
Cure-All	7		
Generous			4
Small			5
Large			5
Harmful			6

Section 1

1. B (exposited: *explain*)

(A) rebutted: *argue against*
(C) disdained: *hate*
(D) foiled: *stop*
(E) debased: *make worse*

2. E (glum: *depressed*)

(A) tonic: *exciting*
(B) myopic: *unclear*
(C) assured: *sure*
(D) stalwart: *strong*

3. B (ensconced: *secure*)

(A) faltered: *unsteady*
(C) corroded: *make worse*
(D) distended: *make large / swell*
(E) prattled: *talkative*

4. C (unassailable: *strong*)

(A) belligerent: *unfriendly*
(B) sagacious: *smart*
(D) frank: *honest*
(E) nefarious: *wicked*

5. E (obtuse: *stupid*)

(A) demure: *shy*
(B) nettlesome: *brave*
(C) diabolical: *wicked*
(D) jovial: *cheerful*

6. E (equanimity: *fair*)

(A) obsequiousness: *flatter*
(B) obduracy: *stubborn*
(C) iconoclasm: *different / odd*
(D) bombast: *arrogant*

7. A (panacea: *cure-all*)

(B) virulence: *harmful*
(C) discourse: *examine*
(D) mosaic: *made from small pieces*
(E) quagmire: *stuck*

8. C (refined...callow: *experienced...inexperienced*)

(A) altruistic...fledgling:
   generous...inexperienced
(B) avaricious...impregnable:
   greedy...strong
(D) decrepit...acceding:
   weak...obedient
(E) seasoned...avant-garde:
   experienced...original

Section 2

1. D (repugnant: *offensive*)

(A) lithe: *flexible*
(B) unprecedented: *original*
(C) blighted: *destroyed*
(E) threadbare: *poor*

2. B (heralded: *praise*)

(A) abominated: *hate*
(C) excoriated: *criticize*
(D) perverted: *make worse*
(E) distended: *make large*

3. B (divergent: *different*)

(A) consecrated: *blessed*
(C) rapturous: *cheerful*
(D) lugubrious: *depressed*
(E) impuissant: *weak*

4. C (jejune: *boring*)

(A) docile: *obedient*
(B) whimsical: *impulsive*
(D) adroit: *skilled*
(E) avant-garde: *original*

5. B (candid…meretricious: *honest…false / lying*)

(A) ineluctable…inept:
    sure…unskilled
(C) pellucid…reckless:
    clear…impulsive
(D) galvanic…acquiescent:
    exciting…obedient
(E) quotidian…caviling:
    ordinary / clichéd…unfriendly

Section 3

1. B (efface: *erase*)

(A) meander: *wander*
(C) stupefy: *surprised*
(D) swagger: *arrogant*
(E) aggregate: *together*

2. D (sumptuous: *rich / extravagant*)

(A) scant: *a little / insufficient*
(B) munificent: *generous*
(C) incontrovertible: *true*
(E) fallacious: *false / lying*

3. B (cogent: *relevant*)

(A) immaterial: *irrelevant*
(C) commodious: *large*
(D) intractable: *stubborn*
(E) malignant: *harmful*

4. C (eleemosynary: *generous*)

(A) laconic: *tight-lipped*
(B) loquacious: *talkative*
(D) malevolent: *wicked*
(E) inept: *unskilled*

5. C (paltry…prodigious:
   ***small…large*)**

(A) pertinacious…assured:
   stubborn…sure
(B) banal…limpid:
   clichéd…clear
(D) petty…soporific:
   insignificant…boring
(E) feeble…appraising:
   weak…questioning

6. C (baleful: *harmful*)

(A) discursive: *irrelevant*
(B) cynical: *questioning*
(D) adamant: *stubborn*
(E) trite: *clichéd*

SAT VOCABULARY PRACTICE TEST 9

Suggested Time: 5 minutes
8 Questions

> **Directions:** In context, choose the word(s) that fits the sentence best.

1. Kevin marveled at the ----- of the snowflake, which had melted upon his finger in less time than it takes to blink.

   (A) ineluctability   (B) pettiness
      (C) perniciousness   (D) evanescence
      (E) wariness

2. The subject of climate change was not considered to be ----- at the international baker's convention, which focused primarily on recipes and business strategies.

   (A) deferential   (B) apropos   (C) buoyant
      (D) elliptical   (E) voracious

3. The very first poet to use pyrrhic hexameter, Luciano Enzo Giancarlo Biscotti nonetheless had to wait more than 600 years to gain recognition as a ----- poet.

   (A) rapacious   (B) vanguard   (C) penurious
      (D) specious   (E) cogent

4. The manager's ----- wardrobe belied an extroverted personality that allowed her to make friends almost effortlessly wherever she went.

   (A) whimsical   (B) innovative   (C) malleable
      (D) demure   (E) surmountable

5. The worker received a clean bill of health from the company doctor, yet he continued to feel too fragile and ----- to even get out of bed, let alone work.

   (A) nonmalignant   (B) insolvent   (C) feeble
      (D) confounded   (E) transient

6. Reporters were stunned when the normally ----- athlete burst into tears during the interview.

   (A) stolid   (B) avaricious   (C) ignominious
      (D) acrid   (E) groundbreaking

7. While his analysis was by no means ----- or original, neither was it entirely -----.

   (A) enduring…seasoned
   (B) prudent…odious
   (C) apocryphal…infinitesimal
   (D) trenchant…insuperable
   (E) groundbreaking...banal

8. He was an unrepentant -----, who made no apologies for spending with total abandon.

   (A) profligate   (B) neophyte   (C) charlatan
      (D) advocate   (E) mercenary

Suggested Time: 3 minutes
5 Questions

> **Directions:** In context, choose the word(s) that fits the sentence best.

1. The current average lifespan of humans is -----, never having reached this level in the past.

   (A) aggregate　(B) steadfast　(C) arable
   　　(D) unprecedented　(E) pernicious

2. While she had expected some intransigence, Paula remained ----- by the level of resistance to her theory that dinosaurs could be genetically replicated and reproduced in the modern world.

   (A) vexed　(B) assuaged　(C) duped
   　　(D) surreptitious　(E) hailed

3. JiHee glanced at the pickled pig snout with ----- before she contemptuously shoved the plate away from her place at the table.

   (A) abatement　(B) serendipity　(C) disdain
   　　(D) elation　(E) impediment

4. When the usually docile horse suddenly brooked Juri's commands to move forward, she wondered about the animal's ----- behavior, until she finally spotted the fire that loomed ahead.

   (A) fractious　(B) baneful　(C) banal
   　　(D) benign　(E) retiring

5. Although he had originally been awed by the celebrity's status, he soon grew tired of her during an interview in which she ----- incessantly, speaking non-stop about matter that were trivial, at best.

   (A) contracted　(B) husbanded　(C) tergiversatec
   　　(D) prattled　(E) flagged

Suggested Time: 4 minutes
6 Questions

Directions: In context, choose the word(s) that fits the sentence best.

1. Although the wildfires appeared to be in -----, firefighters maintained a vigilant watch on the shrinking flames.

    (A) anachronism (B) perniciousness (C) surfeit
       (D) remission   (E) trepidation

2. Jone could not countenance the ----- and so he dedicated his professional life to expunging all the ----- and clichés that he found in manuscripts.

    (A) perspicuity…cornucopias
    (B) banal…platitudes
    (C) exhilarating…insolvencies
    (D) bromide…encomiums
    (E) indomitable…apathies

3. When Mimi's favorite music player dropped down the sewer drain, she was not just disappointed but ----- to the point of tears and wailing.

    (A) apropos (B) miserly (C) dismayed
       (D) jovial   (E) languid

4. No matter how much he disagreed with his superior's decision, the ------ continued to praise her every move to the point of obsequiousness.

    (A) lackey   (B) skeptic   (C) profligate
       (D) reprobate   (E) fiend

5. The ambassador's refusal to attend the reception was interpreted not just as a failure of accepted practice but as ----- and a slight that would long be remembered and damage relations.

    (A) an immoderation   (B) an aberration
       (C) a deprivation   (D) an obloquy
          (E) an animadversion

6. Though he had once possessed a series of ----- positions, for which he was well-paid, he nevertheless found himself a ----- after he invested in a string of fraudulent companies.

    (A) sanctified…philanthropist
    (B) sumptuous…reprobate
    (C) diffident…glutton
    (D) amiable…profligate
    (E) remunerative…pauper

Practice Test 9
Answer Key and Explanations

Section 1

1. (D) evanescence
2. (B) apropos
3. (B) vanguard
4. (D) demure
5. (C) feeble
6. (A) stolid
7. (E) groundbreaking...banal
8. (A) profligate

Section 2

1. (D) unprecedented
2. (A) vexed
3. (C) disdain
4. (A) fractious
5. (D) prattled

Section 3

1. (D) remission
2. (B) banal…platitudes
3. (C) dismayed
4. (A) lackey
5. (D) an obloquy
6. (E) remunerative…pauper

Finding Your Percentile Rank

Raw score: Total Number Right – [Total Number Wrong ÷ 4] = _____

Raw Score	Percentile Rank
19	99
18	97
17	93
16	89
15	85
14	80
13	75
12	70
11	65
10	60
9	50
8	45
7	40
6	35
5	30
4	25
3	20
2	15
1	10
0	5
-1 or below	1 - 4

Identifying Strengths and Areas for Improvement

Go back to the test and circle the questions that you answered incorrectly. This review will allow you to see what vocabulary to study more closely. It will also allow you to see what word lists you need to review more carefully. You can also reference *Score-Raising Vocabulary Builder for ACT and SAT Prep*, a companion study guide and vocabulary workbook.

	Section 1	Section 2	Section 3
Shy	4		
Depressed			3
Short-Lived	1		
Weak	5		
Stubborn		4	
Relevant	2		
Using a Lot	8		
Annoyed		2	
Dislike / Hate		3	
To Flatter			4
To Insult			5
Unemotional	6		
Talkative		5	
Different / Odd			
Original	3, 7	1	
Clichéd	7		2
Retreat			1
Rich			6
Poor			6

Section 1

1. D (evanescence: *short-lived*)

(A) ineluctability: *sure*
(B) pettiness: *insignificant*
(C) perniciousness: *harmful*
(E) wariness: *shy*

2. B (apropos: *relevant*)

(A) deferential: *obedient*
(C) buoyant: *cheerful*
(D) elliptical: *tight-lipped*
(E) voracious: *using a lot*

3. B (vanguard: *original*)

(A) rapacious: *greedy*
(C) penurious: *poor*
(D) specious: *false*
(E) cogent: *relevant*

4. D (demure: *shy*)

(A) whimsical: *impulsive*
(B) innovative: *original*
(C) malleable: *obedient*
(E) surmountable: *weak*

5. C (feeble: *weak*)

(A) nonmalignant: *harmless*
(B) insolvent: *poor*
(D) confounded: *confused*
(E) transient: *short-lived*

6. A (stolid: *unemotional*)

(B) avaricious: *greedy*
(C) ignominious: *shameful*
(D) acrid: *bitter*
(E) groundbreaking: *original*

7. E (groundbreaking...banal: *original...clichéd*)

(A) enduring...seasoned:
    long-lived...experienced
(B) prudent...odious:
    cautious...hate
(C) apocryphal...infinitesimal:
    false / lying...small
(D) trenchant...insuperable:
    relevant...strong

8. A (profligate: *using a lot*)

(B) neophyte: *inexperienced*
(C) charlatan: *fake*
(D) advocate: *argue for*
(E) mercenary: *concerned with objects*

Section 2

1. D (unprecedented: *original*)

(A) aggregate: *together*
(B) steadfast: *same*
(C) arable: *farmable*
(E) pernicious: *harmful*

2. A (vexed: *annoyed*)

(B) assuaged: *make better*
(C) duped: *stupid*
(D) surreptitious: *secret*
(E) hailed: *praise*

3. C (disdain: *hate*)

(A) abatement: *stop*
(B) serendipity: *lucky*
(D) elation: *cheerful*
(E) impediment: *stop*

4. A (fractious: *stubborn*)

(B) baneful: *harmful*
(C) banal: *clichéd*
(D) benign: *harmless*
(E) retiring: *obedient*

5. D (prattle: *talkative*)

(A) contracted: *make small*
(B) husbanded: *using a little*
(C) tergiversated: *false / lying*
(E) flagged: *stop*

Section 3

1. D (remission: *retreat*)

(A) anachronism: *old*
(B) perniciousness: *harmful*
(C) surfeit: *a lot*
(E) trepidation: *afraid*

2. B (banal...platitudes: *clichéd...clichéd*)

(A) perspicuity...cornucopias: *clear...a lot*
(C) exhilarating...insolvencies: *exciting...poor*
(D) bromide...encomiums: *clichéd...praise*
(E) indomitable...apathies: *strong...indifferent*

3. C (dismayed: *depressed*)

(A) apropos: *relevant*
(B) miserly: *greedy*
(D) jovial: *cheerful*
(E) languid: *lazy / indifferent*

4. A (lackey: *flatter*)

(B) skeptic: *questioning*
(C) profligate: *using a lot*
(D) reprobate: *wicked*
(E) fiend: *wicked*

5. D (an obloquy: *insult*)

(A) an immoderation: *using a lot*
(B) an aberration: *different*
(C) a deprivation: *little / insufficient*
(E) an animadversion: *hate*

6. E (remunerative...pauper:
   rich...poor)

(A) sanctified...philanthropist:
    blessed...generous
(B) sumptuous...reprobate:
    extravagant...wicked
(C) diffident...glutton:
    shy...greedy
(D) amiable...profligate:
    friendly...using a lot

SAT VOCABULARY PRACTICE TEST 10

Suggested Time: 5 minutes
8 Questions

Directions: In context, choose the word(s) that fits the sentence best.

1. Upon the revelation that it had covertly supported treachery, the country's relationship with its neighbor immediately transformed from ----- to hostile.

   (A) amiable   (B) bracing   (C) novice
      (D) feeble   (E) disputatious

2. Due to the embarrassment that it caused her, Gina wished that her father was not so ----- about his love for science fiction shows, which he proudly displayed by dressing up as his favorite characters.

   (A) peculiar   (B) incredulous   (C) derisive
      (D) conspicuous   (E) deleterious

3. Instead of engaging in the conversational ----- expected in the forum, the professor instead launched into a long-winded, ----- monologue.

   (A) discourse...bombastic
   (B) consummation...trenchant
   (C) panacea...profligate
   (D) catalogue...prudent
   (E) mosaic...obsequious

4. Amidst the ornate, exquisite furniture and urbane artworks of the hotel lobby, the shiny lawn chairs and picnic tables remained nothing, if not, -----.

   (A) lavish   (B) intractable   (C) malapropos
      (D) banal   (E) detrimental

5. Placed beside the gargantuan figure of Jupiter in the model of the solar system, the Earth appeared to be ----- planet whose size was insignificant.

   (A) an ephemeral   (B) an imperishable
      (C) an intemperate   (D) a bantam
         (E) a gargantuan

6. Brown was alternately lauded and excoriated for his opinionated, ----- criticisms of democracy's institutions, which he alone stated.

   (A) profligate   (B) stolid   (C) iconoclastic
      (D) faltering   (E) corrosive

7. Had she known the full pestilence present in the garbage dumps, she never would have chosen to ----- her research project on modern landfills but instead would have chosen a less ----- topic such as flowers or perfume.

    (A) terminate…benign
    (B) commence…unequivocal
    (C) disparage…deleterious
    (D) institute…pellucid
    (E) inaugurate…noxious

8. In contrast to the ephemeral discomfort caused by a headache, the intense pain of a migraine seems ----- to those who suffer from them.

    (A) potent   (B) voracious   (C) trifling
       (D) interminable   (E) remunerative

Suggested Time: 3 minutes
5 Questions

Directions: In context, choose the word(s) that fits the sentence best.

1. No one who knows of genocide and does nothing can escape -----; each person shares in the blame.

   (A) discrepancy   (B) culpability   (C) anachronism
       (D) remission   (E) veracity

2. On Friars Day queens in England traditionally wore sackcloth not because they were ----- and couldn't afford finery but because they wanted to demonstrate their piousness.

   (A) impecunious   (B) forthright   (C) erudite
       (D) slight   (E) beneficent

3. The architect's plans were meant to be -----, never apparent to pedestrians or anyone else not immediately involved in the restoration process.

   (A) impecunious   (B) blunt   (C) immaterial
       (D) trenchant   (E) unobtrusive

4. Although the professor had was known to be ----- in the classroom, his conversations outside of it were crystal clear and easy to understand.

   (A) belligerent   (B) recondite   (C) amoral
       (D) effusive   (E) laconic

5. Normally gregarious at such social events, Sheila surprised her colleagues when she remained ---- throughout the entire party, refusing to talk to a single person.

   (A) docile   (B) capricious   (C) blithe
       (D) feeble   (E) diffident

Suggested Time: 4 minutes
6 Questions

> **Directions:** In context, choose the word(s) that fits the sentence best.

1. Stalin possessed such a ----- appetite for porcelain figurines that advisors worried about its potentially harmful, ----- effect on his leadership.

   (A) corpulent…repugnant
   (B) tenacious…munificent
   (C) dilatory...blighting
   (D) replete…amorphous
   (E) ravenous…pernicious

2. The parents reprimanded their child after she thoughtlessly ran across the street without looking, explaining to her that such ----- act could cause her serious injury.

   (A) a confounding   (B) an ephemeral
      (C) a heedless   (D) an imperishable
         (E) a spendthrift

3. Though it had been proven on other occasions, Inky's reputation for ----- was belied when, rather than pursue the strange noise outside of the house, he ran to the furthest room and hid under the sofa.

   (A) glumness   (B) asceticism   (C) amicability
      (D) stoutheartedness   (E) truncation

4. While she professed to be ----- chess player in her college application, Elizabeth's true ----- towards the game was manifested by the fact that she never played a single match while at school.

   (A) a callow…superciliousness
   (B) an avid…insouciance
   (C) a ductile…wariness
   (D) an elliptical…tumescence
   (E) a nefarious…keenness

5. The government regime was charged with ----- genocide, after it urged members, through television and radio broadcasts, to take up arms against another ethnic group.

   (A) inciting   (B) debunking   (C) curtailing
      (D) chastising   (E) adulterating

6. Paradoxically, the amount of meals purchased at fast-food restaurants ----- during economic downturns instead of decreasing.

   (A) extirpates   (B) sullies   (C) waxes
      (D) inaugurates   (E) elucidates

Practice Test 10
Answer Key and Explanations

Section 1

1. (A) amiable
2. (D) conspicuous
3. (A) discourse...bombastic
4. (C) malapropos
5. (D) a bantam
6. (C) iconoclastic
7. (E) inaugurate…noxious
8. (D) interminable

Section 2

1. (B) culpability
2. (A) impecunious
3. (E) unobtrusive
4. (B) recondite
5. (E) diffident

Section 3

1. (E) ravenous…pernicious
2. (C) a heedless
3. (D) stoutheartedness
4. (B) an avid…insouciance
5. (A) inciting
6. (C) waxes

Finding Your Percentile Rank

Raw score: Total Number Right – [Total Number Wrong ÷ 4] = _____

Raw Score	Percentile Rank
19	99
18	97
17	93
16	89
15	85
14	80
13	75
12	70
11	65
10	60
9	50
8	45
7	40
6	35
5	30
4	25
3	20
2	15
1	10
0	5
-1 or below	1 - 4

Identifying Strengths and Areas for Improvement

Go back to the test and circle the questions that you answered incorrectly. This review will allow you to see what vocabulary to study more closely. It will also allow you to see what word lists you need to review more carefully. You can also reference *Score-Raising Vocabulary Builder for ACT and SAT Prep*, a companion study guide and vocabulary workbook.

	Section 1	Section 2	Section 3
To Start	7		5
Impulsive			2
Friendly	1		
Small	5		
Not Obvious		3	
Arrogant	3		
Passionate			4
Poor		2	
Obvious	2		
Harmful	7		1
Shy		5	
Discuss	3		
Long-Lived	8		
Irrelevant	4		
Worthy of Blame		1	
Brave			3
Different / Odd	6		
Greedy			1
Difficult to Understand		4	
Indifferent			4
Make Large			6

Section 1

1. A (amiable: *friendly*)

(B) bracing: *exciting*
(C) novice: *inexperienced*
(D) feeble: *weak*
(E) disputatious: *unfriendly*

2. D (conspicuous: *obvious*)

(A) peculiar: *different / odd*
(B) incredulous: *questioning*
(C) derisive: *insult*
(E) deleterious: *harmful*

3. A (discourse…bombastic: *discuss…arrogant*)

(B) consummation…trenchant: *finish…relevant*
(C) panacea…profligate: *cure-all…using a lot*
(D) catalogue…prudent: *to record…cautious*
(E) mosaic…obsequious: *made from small pieces…flatter*

4. C (malapropos: *irrelevant*)

(A) lavish: *rich / extravagant*
(B) intractable: *stubborn*
(D) banal: *clichéd*
(E) detrimental: *harmful*

5. D (a bantam: *little*)

(A) an ephemeral: *short-lived*
(B) an imperishable: *long-lived*
(C) an intemperate: *using a lot*
(E) a gargantuan: *large*

6. C (iconoclastic: *different / odd*)

(A) profligate: *using a lot*
(B) stolid: *unemotional*
(D) faltering: *unsteady*
(E) corrosive: *make worse*

7. E (inaugurate…noxious: *start…harmful*)

(A) terminate…benign: *finish…harmless*
(B) commence…unequivocal: *start…sure*
(C) disparage…deleterious: *insult…harmful*
(D) institute…pellucid: *start…clear*

8. D (interminable: *long-lived*)

(A) potent: *strong*
(B) voracious: *greedy*
(C) trifling: *small*
(E) remunerative: *rich*

Section 2

1. B (culpability: *worthy of blame*)

(A) discrepancy: *different*
(C) anachronism: *old*
(D) remission: *retreat*
(E) veracity: *true*

2. A (impecunious: *poor*)

(B) forthright: *honest*
(C) erudite: *smart*
(D) slight: *insult*
(E) beneficent: *generous*

3. E (unobtrusive: *not obvious*)

(A) impecunious: *poor*
(B) blunt: *honest*
(C) immaterial: *irrelevant*
(D) trenchant: *relevant*

4. B (recondite: *difficult to understand*)

(A) belligerent: *unfriendly*
(C) amoral: *wicked*
(D) effusive: *talkative*
(E) laconic: *tight-lipped*

5. E (diffident: *shy*)

(A) docile: *obedient*
(B) capricious: *impulsive*
(C) blithe: *cheerful*
(D) feeble: *weak*

Section 3

1. E (ravenous...pernicious: *greedy...harmful*)

(A) corpulent...repugnant: *large...offensive*
(B) tenacious...munificent: *stubborn...generous*
(C) dilatory...blighting: *late...destroyed*
(D) replete...amorphous: *a lot...shapeless*

2. C (heedless: *impulsive*)

(A) a confounding: *confused*
(B) an ephemeral: *short-lived*
(D) an imperishable: *long-lived*
(E) a spendthrift: *using a lot*

3. D (stoutheartedness: *brave*)

(A) glumness: *depressed*
(B) asceticism: *using a little*
(C) amicability: *friendly*
(E) truncation: *make small*

4. B (an avid...insouciance: *passionate...indifferent*)

(A) a callow...superciliousness: *inexperienced...arrogant*
(C) a ductile...wariness: *obedient...shy*
(D) an elliptical...tumescence: *tight-lipped...make large*
(E) a nefarious...keenness: *wicked...smart*

5. A (inciting: *start*)

(B) debunking: *argue against*
(C) curtailing: *stop*
(D) chastising: *criticize / scold*
(E) adulterating: *make worse*

6. C (waxes: *make large*)

(A) extirpates: *stop*
(B) sullies: *make worse*
(D) inaugurates: *start*
(E) elucidates: *explain*

OTHER TITLES AVAILABLE FROM FUSION PRESS

SAT Practice Test (Kindle Edition)

5 SAT Math Practice Tests

5 SAT Critical Reading Practice Tests

5 SAT Writing Practice Tests

10 SAT Vocabulary Practice Tests

5 Fantastically Hard SAT Math Practice Tests

5 Fantastically Hard SAT Critical Reading Practice Tests

5 Fantastically Hard SAT Writing Practice Tests

5 PSAT Math Practice Tests

5 PSAT Writing Practice Tests

10 PSAT Vocabulary Practice Tests

5 Fantastically Hard PSAT Math Practice Tests

5 Fantastically Hard PSAT Critical Reading Practice Tests

5 Fantastically Hard PSAT Writing Practice Tests

10 Fantastically Hard PSAT Vocabulary Practice Tests

Score-Raising Vocabulary Builder for ACT and SAT Prep (Level 1)

Score-Raising Vocabulary Builder for ACT and SAT Prep (Level 2)

CPSIA information can be obtained at www.ICGtesting.com
Printed in the USA
LVOW09s0712170813

348222LV00001B/1/P